Growing Your Garden The Earth-Friendly Way

Growing Your Garden The Earth-Friendly Way

Garden Columns from

The Christian Science Monitor

Written by PETER TONGE

The Christian Science Publishing Society

Boston, Massachusetts, U.S.A.

Growing Your Garden The Earth-Friendly Way is an expanded edition of
The Good Green Garden, Peter Tonge's earlier work published in 1979.

ISBN: 0-87510-210-7
Library of Congress Catalog Card Number: 93-71358

Printed in the United States of America

Design: Nieshoff Design
Photography: Bill Grant (unless otherwise noted)

Text is printed on recycled paper.

*To Barbara, whose talents in the kitchen add
immeasurably to the joy of gardening*

Contents

Preface   *xiii*

Soil Building   2

    How to Turn Sticky Clay into Garden Soil in Just
      One Season

    How to Enlist the Aid of Earthworms in Your Soil-
      building Program

Composting   8

    Making Rich Compost

    They're Growing Bacteria to Make Rich Black
      Humus

    Red Wrigglers for Indoor Composting

    Kitchen Composter Turns Scraps to Fertilizer

    An Easy Way to Compost?—Try Digging a Ditch

    Fertilizer and Compost from a Plastic Bag

    Simple Appliance Makes Short Work of
      Fallen Leaves

Fertilizer   22

    Soil-Test Kits—Invaluable

    Good Fertilizer—a Mix of Chemicals and Compost

    Fireplace Can Cut Fuel Bill—and Fertilize Garden

    Put Seaweed in Your Soil for Bigger Harvests

    Purity Test for Chemical Fertilizers

Mulching   32

    Mulch: Security Blanket for Your Garden

    Determined Mulching Can Keep Slugs Away

Gardening Techniques   **38**

     Taking the Spadework Out of Gardening

     Is No-Dig Gardening Better?

     A No-Dig Garden with the Help of Plastic

     Old French Method Yields Supergarden

     Microfarming for the Backyard or Forest Clearing

     Hay-Bale Beds Are Fertile Alternative to Stony
       Ground

     Roots on the Rooftop with Shallow-Bed Gardens

     Planting in Broad Rows Uses Garden Space Best

     How to Make Part of Your Garden Grow All Winter

     French-Intensive Gardening from a "New" Old Book

     Raising Plants on a Liquid Diet

     "King-size" Gardens from Postage-Stamp Plots

     Gardening by the Square Foot

Greenhouses   **64**

     Helping Your Hothouse Hold onto Its Heat

     Sloping Greenhouse Beats Soaring Winter Costs

     Homemade Greenhouse Yields Crops All Winter

Seeds   **70**

     Don't Throw Out Those Leftover Seeds—Yet

     How to Keep Old Seed So It Will Grow in the
       Spring

General   **74**

     Figuring Out How Much Your Garden Will Grow

     Making the Most of Your Produce

     How a Diary Helps to Plan Your Garden

     With Notes in Hand, Plan Next Year's Garden

     Friendly Toads Feast on Pests

     Bats Battle Bugs

     How to Start Seeds Indoors—and Save

Crops   90

      Beans—One of the Easiest and Most Productive Crops

      Unearthed: Gardening Secrets for Better Beets

      Pampered Broccoli Will Reward You Well

      Cabbage Patch of Which Mrs. Wiggs Could Be Proud

      Cabbages That Just Won't Quit

      Harvesting Carrots All Year

      A More Efficient Cauliflower Gains Ground

      Garden Too Small for Corn? Don't You Believe It

      High Time to Start Growing the Lowly Cucumber

      Hothouses for Cucumbers from Old Auto Tires

      Every Gardener Needs Herbs

      Leeks—Worth Cost, Effort: the Gourmet's Onion

      Lettuce Grows Best in Soft Nitrogen-Rich Soil

      Raising a Bushel of Onions in Your Backyard

      An Easier Way to Plant Onions

      For a Long-Running Onion Try Planting Egyptians

      Parsnips—a Hardy, Tasty Garden Crop

      How to Grow a Bumper Crop of Peas

      How to Grow Peas with a Minimum of Fuss

      Try Growing Potatoes on or above the Ground

      Volunteer Vine Inspires Sugar Pumpkin Crop

      Year-Round Garden Supplies Yule Rutabaga

      How Kitchen Waste Boosts Squash Harvest

      Try Sweet Potatoes—in the Garden and on the Menu

      Caged Tomato Plants Produce Bountiful Crop

      How to Double Your Tomato Yield—the Japanese Way

      Don't Turn Up Your Nose at Rhubarb

      Raspberries, Red and Black, and How to Grow Them

      Backyard Strawberry Patch Needs Water, Sun, and Care

      Alpine Strawberries—a Great Border Plant

Afterword   143

Photographs

❧

Starting out	P-1
Future promise	P-2 and 3
Strong roots	P-4
Nature's tillers	P-4
Transplants at the ready	P-4 and 5
From the kitchen into the garden	P-6 and 7
Sweet carrots	P-8 and 9
Gourmet leeks	P-9
Peppers aplenty	P-10
Cuke-laden vines	P-11
Caged tomatoes	P-12
Washbasin turnips	P-12
Bountiful beans	P-12 and 13
The "back forty"	P-14 and 15
Abundant harvest	P-16
Tools of the trade	P-16

Preface

When the editors of *The Christian Science Monitor* first asked me to write a regular garden column, I returned a flat-out no. I had gardened avidly since my late teens and was pretty good at it. But I knew enough to know that I didn't know anywhere near enough to be considered an expert on the topic. Then two things happened within a week that made me change my mind.

First, my wife and I were walking through some display gardens when we overheard a woman ask her companion: "What are those?" Since he couldn't answer, I turned and said: "Those, madam, are carrots."

"Carrots?" she responded, "Carrots? Do they grow in the ground?" It seems she thought they were picked from a bush like tomatoes or peppers.

The second incident was closer to home. Earlier in the year, I had shown a young neighbor how to plant potatoes and watched with satisfaction as they grew into large healthy vines. So it came as a surprise in the early fall when she told me how disappointing the crop had been. They had yielded only a few tiny potatoes, she said, "when I pulled up the vines."

Ascertaining that she really had pulled and not dug them up, I called for a garden fork and sank it deep into the soft, rich soil. What broke through the surface as I pulled back on the handle was a generous supply of creamy white tubers, ranging from golf-ball size all the way up to large bakers. The harvest was a success by any yardstick.

It was at that moment that I knew I could write a regular garden column. While there was so much about gardening that I still did not know, it was also obvious that I knew a whole lot more than many people out there who were hungering for information. In any event, I could always call on the experts—the trained horticulturists, the university professors, and the extension agents—when the need arose.

And so the column began, based on personal experiences with growing plants and the experiences of other home gardeners, interlaced every so often with interviews with recognized experts.

It was an approach that appealed to readers and one that makes this book, which is basically a collection of columns as they appeared in the *Monitor,* different from many others. While it is a how-to book, it's not a textbook. Rather, it's a collection of anecdotes in which gardeners say what they did, how they did it, and with what results. The hope is that readers will take the ideas they contain, evaluate them, and apply them to their own gardens if they feel so inclined.

Many of these columns first appeared in the book *The Good Green Garden* published by Harpswell Press several years ago. In this book they have been updated where necessary, and new ones, like one on shallow-bed gardening and another on growing in hay bales, have been added to provide readers with a more complete range of gardening options. Color photographs, all taken in my own garden, also add a pleasing measure of interest to the book.

From time to time in this book you may read statements like "dig compost into the top six inches of soil." They reflect my thinking at the time they were written and are still valid. But my own preference these days is for no-dig gardening. In fact, I haven't turned the soil in my garden for better than ten years (see articles on no-dig gardening), except for lifting potatoes or harvesting other root crops. I simply spread compost or other amendments on top of the soil and let the earthworms do the digging. Works beautifully!

May the ideas contained in this book work beautifully in your garden, too. I see no reason why they shouldn't.

Peter Tonge
Weymouth, Massachusetts
July 1993

Growing Your Garden The Earth-Friendly Way

Soil Building

Good soil is a gardener's most-valued resource. With it, you can husband relatively few seeds into an abundant harvest. Without it, your garden can be a source of chronic frustration.

So, if you don't have first-rate soil to begin with, your first priority should be to build up the soil and then to manage it as the major working capital of your garden.

No matter what soil type you start with, brick hard or as sandy as a Cape Cod beach, you can build up a beautiful loam that virtually will guarantee good harvests.

It's fairly simple really. You dig in organic matter—leaves, hay, weeds, garden waste, and kitchen scraps. Lots of it.

Once mixed into your garden, such matter quickly breaks down into soil-building, moisture-storing, nutrient-rich humus, sometimes referred to as the "fat of the land."

How to Turn Sticky Clay into Garden Soil in Just One Season

Two decades ago Leandre and Gretchen Poisson began carving a family food garden out of an acre or so of New England forest. But

when they finally hauled away the last of the giant pine stumps, all but a few crumbs of the paper-thin topsoil had been dragged with them.

What remained was a sticky yellow clay that was about as appetizing to the potatoes, carrots, and other food crops they planned to grow as a stick of chalk is to a hungry man.

Yet today that yellow clay, which I saw for myself in a more recently cleared area, is a deep red-brown color and as soft as velvet to the touch. It is a nutrient-rich, moisture-holding growing medium in which all crops thrive. As a result, theirs is always a well-filled larder.

Immediate Soil

Soil building is the key to any garden's success. The need, then, was to get humus into the soil as quickly as possible or, as Mrs. Poisson expresses it, "to establish the conditions in which the microorganisms that nourish the plants can thrive."

Impressively, they built that soil into "reasonable shape" almost immediately and by fall were "buried in eggplant and cantaloupe," to quote Mrs. Poisson.

How was such "instant soil" possible? For the Poissons the answer lay in rotting hay, stable and chicken manure by the ton, and a single application of limestone (to correct acidity), rock minerals (for phosphate and potassium), and basic slag (for trace elements). These ingredients were all turned into the soil with a rotary cultivator, left for a few weeks, and then planted to crops.

The best time to start a garden is in the fall, says Mrs. Poisson: "Turn the organic matter into the soil and leave it to break down over the winter." But "you can start a garden any time," she insists.

The Recipe

This is the Poisson recipe for soil building: Till the soil lightly once; then spread phosphate rock (for phosphate), granite dust (for potassium), and basic slag (for trace elements), all at 1 pound per 10 square feet of garden, plus limestone at a rate recommended by the soil test, and till again. Next, spread the manure, including nitrogen-rich chicken manure, an inch or more thick if you have it over the bed, along with several inches of rotting hay. Till again until the ingredients are thoroughly mixed in.

In this situation the microorganisms readily break down the materials into humus-filled soil.

For straw you can use leaves; green sand substitutes for granite dust, seaweed or seaweed solution for basic slag, and cottonseed meal or feather meal for chicken manure.

Soil building is a continuous process at the Poisson farm. This means tilling in organic materials in the spring, digging in residue as a crop is harvested, and turning in more material again in the fall. In addition, the Poissons mulch their beds with hay once the soil has warmed up, and this, too, continues to break down slowly and nourish the soil.

Time Lag Is Out

What the Poissons have found is that as their garden soil has improved, so has its appetite. By this they mean that as the soil's microorganism population has increased, so has the speed at which it is able to convert organic materials into soil. Put another way, the time lag between a leaf being tilled into the soil and its turning into plant nutrients has been dramatically cut.

The Poissons place newspaper (five sheets thick) down on all paths between the garden beds and cover it with stable bedding. All year long it slowly biodegrades. Come spring, it is all turned into the beds and new materials placed on the paths.

"The trick with feeding your soil," says Lee Poisson, "is never to stop."

More Soil-building Options

One proven way to build soil fertility is to spread leaves, straw, and other plant waste to a depth of 12 inches each fall and then rototill it all in.

But what if you cannot get such quantities? And what if your garden is too small to warrant hiring a tiller? Well, you might start as I did many years ago.

First, dig a trench about 6 inches deep and as long as you want your garden to be. For convenience, make the trench as wide as your spade. Each evening take the day's collection of kitchen scraps, plus lawn clippings, and throw it into one end of the trench. Fill the trench to the top, and then add a 2-inch cover of earth.

When the whole trench is filled and covered this way, it becomes a row to plant in. Then start a second row.

You might try digging individual holes, perhaps a foot or more deep, for such widely spaced plants as tomatoes. When setting out plants in these rows or holes, be sure the roots are surrounded by soil. Let them grow into the waste as it breaks down.

Balanced Fertilizers

Try liquefying the food waste in a kitchen blender if you are concerned about attracting unwanted animal visitors to the garden. Grinding the waste in a meat grinder can help, too.

In any event, you probably will need to boost production by the application of balanced fertilizers during the first few years of gardening.

Once you've built up the soil, you can keep it in good shape relatively easily. For instance, I seldom dig anything into my soils anymore. I simply spread the compost or ground leaves around the plants and let it steadily decompose into the soil.

How to Enlist the Aid of Earthworms in Your Soil-building Program

Did you know that there is a natural fertilizer, virtually free for the asking, that contains 5 times the nitrate, 7 times the available phosphorus, 3 times the exchangeable magnesium, 11 times the potash, and 1½ times the calcium found in the best topsoil in the United States?

It is called worm castings, and the current retail price of this dark gray to black powder is $1.50 a pound. In fact, a growing number of earthworm ranches, or bait farms, are finding that the castings (once considered a waste product) are more valuable to them than the worms themselves.

But you don't need to spend dollars on this "black magic," as some of its more enthusiastic advocates term it. With a little effort you can have it made for you in a backyard worm pit. Or you can encourage the worms right in your garden soil.

Egypt Recalled

The earthworm is said to be one of the reasons the ancient Egyptian civilization flourished for 3,000 years. Billions of earthworms, according to the U.S. Department of Agriculture investigations into the fertility of the Nile Valley, "indicate that the great fertility of the soil in this valley is due in large part to the work of earthworms." The earthworms apparently converted the annual alluvial deposits into "a soil of exceptional richness" ("The Challenge of Earthworm Research," Soil and Health Foundation, Emmaus, PA, 1961).

The active earthworm eats its own weight in organic waste and soil every 24 hours. As this material passes through the worm's digestive tract, both acids and alkalis are neutralized, and soil minerals are converted into a form that is readily available to plants. Hence, the fertilizer value of the casts.

Actinomycetes, organisms that play a major role in decomposing organic matter, also multiply seven times in their journey through the worm.

Then there is the engineering feat of the earthworm—the tunneling that helps the drainage and aeration of the soil. No wonder Charles Darwin, after an extensive study of the worm, said: "It may be doubted whether there are any other animals which have played so important a part in the history of the world than these lowly creatures" (*The Earthworm Book,* Jerry Minuich, Rodale Press).

3 Million Per Acre?

When an earthworm dies, its body decomposes and adds nitrogen to the soil—as much as 1,000 pounds per acre per year in organically rich soil. The average worm population in the United States on moderately good farm and garden soil is about 50,000 to the acre. But populations can exceed several million to the acre. The Good Gardeners' Association in Britain, which follows a no-till, heavy composting policy, estimates its worm population at 3 million to the acre.

The need, then, is to encourage the earthworm to stay in the garden and multiply. In other words, to feed it lavishly so that it has plenty of raw material to convert into fertilizer.

When a bed is being prepared, this can be readily accomplished by digging in compost or manures or both. After plants are up and growing, the task is more difficult, but a considerable worm-feeding program can be continued just the same.

Sifted compost can be spread on the surface of the soil between growing plants. Well-rotted manure can be used the same way. Once your soil has warmed up sufficiently for good growth, you can add a mulch of chopped-up leaves, weeds, and grass cuttings.

Table-Scrap Slurry

Earthworms will come to the surface and feed on mulch as readily as if it is incorporated in the soil. Worms will even eat shredded newspaper; I have seen plenty of evidence of this in my own garden.

You might create a slurry of water and kitchen waste in your blender each evening and apply this around the roots of your plants. The plants will benefit from the water-soluble nutrients immediately available in the slurry, and the worms will quickly process the residue.

An outstanding way to enrich soil and feed earthworms is to dig or rototill fresh green material into the soil. While worms obviously thrive best if left undisturbed, rototilling does not have the devastating effect on them that many fear. My own limited experience with this form of tilling confirms what others have found: worm populations quickly reorganize and establish themselves in a tilled piece of land, apparently thriving on the organic matter that has been introduced into the soil.

Composting

Making Rich Compost

Sam Donatelli of Pittsburgh makes loads of dark, crumbly, sweet-smelling compost out of kitchen waste, leaves, lawn clippings, and weeds to feed an impressive home garden.

In Omaha, James Fix does similar things with wastepaper and cow manure. And in Brockton, Massachusetts, Bob Doroska made some of the best compost I have ever seen (or used) out of sawdust and leather dust.

"Why not?" he says. "If it's organic it can be composted."

Mr. Donatelli makes his compost year-round indoors in the basement of his home. I'm told of other gardeners who operate compost bins on rooftops, porches, and even in dark corner cupboards. Limitations imposed by space and seasons, it seems, are being readily overcome by innovative gardeners.

The plain fact is that composting has caught on all over the United States. "Why waste waste when it can be turned into something beneficial?" is a sentiment with growing appeal. Compost made

from a wide range of garden and other waste is a valuable fertilizer and soil conditioner and also makes economic sense in these days of high commercial fertilizer prices.

Composting is pretty simple, actually. Just mix together a variety of organic materials, dampen them, place them in a pile, and let the bacteria and fungi take it from there. If there is enough nitrogen in the pile, the bacteria will get the job done in a matter of weeks; if not, they'll do it much more slowly, taking 3 to 6 months depending on the time of year.

Green materials (fresh weeds, lawn clippings, kitchen waste) and manures have more than enough nitrogen for fast breakdown; dry cellulose materials (dry grass, dry leaves, sawdust) don't have enough (though dry leaves are much better than sawdust). Hence the need to mix together a variety of different materials.

The heap will quickly tell you if the mixture is right for fast de-composition. If it has not warmed up by the second day, there is not enough nitrogen. If, on the other hand, you smell ammonia coming from the heap, you have too much nitrogen, and the excess is simply being wasted as ammonia gas.

Here is one approach to composting recommended by the University of Vermont Extension Service: Take some wire-mesh fencing between 4 and 5 feet high and about 10 feet long. Fasten the ends together to form a compost cage. Allow for an inch or so of overlap where the ends are fastened together. The cage should be a little over 3 feet in diameter.

Stand the cage on end, and begin filling it with the waste vegetable materials. Start with a 3-inch or so layer of leaves, grass, or garden waste, or a mixture of all of these. Next, add a bucketful of kitchen scraps. (Substitute manure for kitchen waste if you like, or throw in a few handfuls of fertilizer rich in nitrogen, such as blood meal or feather meal.) Then thoroughly moisten, but do not soak, the materials with water.

Continue to build the compost pile this way until you have used up all the waste materials on hand. Always cover the kitchen waste with a layer of leaves. It makes for a neater appearance, and flies are not attracted to the exposed food.

Visit a Lumberyard

A compost heap, built as suggested with an adequate supply of kitchen waste or manures for the drier waste, will heat up considerably within a few days. Temperatures within the heap can reach 150°F as microbes break down the organic matter.

If all you have to compost are kitchen scraps (frequently the case in winter), visit a lumberyard to see if you can get some sawdust. Mix the sawdust and the food waste together in equal parts.

Otherwise, just empty the scraps into the compost cage (they probably will stay frozen most of the time), and in the spring recompost them by mixing with liberal quantities of soil, if no other materials are available.

The compost should be ready for use in 4 to 6 weeks. Use it throughout the garden. If your soil is poor, then dig in some of the compost. Otherwise, spread it on top of the soil. This way it acts as a protective mulch while it steadily releases nutrients into the soil every time it rains.

While it is relatively simple to make a composting cage or bin, the gardening industry has begun turning out models that make the composting area as attractive as it is useful. One is Rotocrop, an upright bin made from individual sliding panels; another is the Earthmaker, a tumbler designed to make regular turning of the compost a simple matter.

Rotocrop had not thought of its product for indoor use, but Mr. Donatelli took his model into the basement so he could make compost in winter. Impressed by his reports, Rotocrop official Graham Kinsman decided to test indoor composting for himself. "It works well," he says with satisfaction.

A feature of the Rotocrop is that it does not have to be filled all at one time.

"Start with at least 12 inches of materials," says Mr. Kinsman, "to provide enough bulk for heating up." Thereafter, add the materials once a week or whenever you have collected enough materials to add a 2- to 3-inch layer at a time. Ultimately, you can be adding fresh material at the top while removing mature compost from the bottom.

I bought a compost tumbler late one fall and just had time to make one good batch of compost before plunging temperatures cut short my home-produced fertilizer program for the season.

I filled my tumbler with shredded leaves (maple, oak, and willow) and kitchen waste in a 3-to-1 ratio. Then I added one bucketful of rabbit manure, which a neighbor kindly let me have, and sprinkled on enough dishwashing water to fill a watering can.

Flanges inside ensure that the compost tumbles as the drum is rotated. I rotated the drum 5 times each day to thoroughly turn the compost. Within two days I had compost too hot for my hand to endure for more than a few moments. In the cool morning air I could see steam drifting out through the two air vents.

This turning method rapidly speeded up decomposition, so that in just 14 days I had compost as good as I had ever made and with a fraction of the previous effort involved.

They're Growing Bacteria to Make Rich Black Humus

A mutual friend introduced me to Judd Ringer at dinner some fifteen years ago, and I quickly realized I had met a rather remarkable man. Around 1970 he gave up the financial security of a successful kitchenware business to begin producing, of all things, bacteria, fungi, molds, and enzymes.

Every day, in vats filled with a nutrient solution, he and microbiologist Don Loveness raised vast armies of microflora destined to go out and conquer the world's vegetative waste—literally chew it up and digest it into the rich black humus that works wonders with garden soil. The Ringer-Loveness composting product— the first of many biological garden aids now turned out by the Ringer corporation of Eden Prairie, Minnesota—turns plain leaves into finished compost in 60 to 90 days. Significantly, this action occurs without the addition of manures, kitchen waste, or green vegetation.

The bacteria necessary for decomposing waste exist everywhere. They are in the soil, the air, and the waste itself; so you can get decomposition without any inoculant. But a rich inoculant, complete with an energy source for the bacteria, can speed things up dramatically.

Leaves on their own, for instance, can take a year or more to break down, compared with the 2 to 3 months with the Ringer compost culture.

Ringer and Loveness first looked into composting leaves after their community, and many others around the country, had banned leaf burning. How could the leaves be induced to break down more speedily? they wanted to know.

Their search for a good mix of microbes to do this work took them to temperate and tropical forests, to farmlands, and to deserts. Soil samples from each area were used as inoculants in piles of leaves.

According to Don Loveness, the results differed widely. Some soil samples decayed the leaves 3 to 4 times more rapidly than others. In the end it was soil from the rich organic farms of the Iowa Amish communities that proved uniformly superior to others. This soil then provided the initial breeding stock for the Ringer culture.

In the Ringer laboratories a culture is introduced into a nutrient solution the way a culture is introduced into milk to make cheese. Millions of tiny air bubbles constantly pass through the solution, providing the bacteria with ample oxygen. Under these optimum conditions, each bacterium reproduces itself every 20 minutes. At the end of 1 hour 1 bacterium has become 8, at the end of 7 hours more than 2 million. My inexpensive calculator refuses to tell me what the 24-hour total could be.

Even the most streamlined kitchenware assembly line could not come close to that sort of productivity, so Judd Ringer went into microflora production full time.

Not content with early results, encouraging as they were, Loveness constantly searched for still more effective decay organisms. At the same time he bred, by selection, improved strains within their own stock.

One strain was developed purely for its enzyme-producing capacity. Much as a farmer keeps a herd of cows for milk, several vats of this strain are maintained purely to "milk" their enzymes, which are then included in the inoculant.

The tenderizer you use on a piece of bargain-basement beef these days is nothing more than enzymes. And enzymes serve the same purpose in a compost pile.

The moment water is added to a compost heap, the microbes in the culture (3½ billion in each gram) are activated. My inoculated heap of shredded leaves dropped 18 inches within a matter of days. Some of this was natural compaction, but much of it was the decay process, too. At the end of 4 days it was boiling hot.

Red Wrigglers for Indoor Composting

Once or twice a week Mary Apelhof dumps her collection of kitchen waste in a small wooden box in the basement of her Kalamazoo, Michigan, home and forgets about it.

If she has her way, she'll get just about everyone else in the land to do the same sort of thing no matter where they live—homes, condos, or one-room efficiencies.

The point is, Mrs. Apelhof, with a master's degree in education to her credit, has developed a very effective, energy-efficient, and simple-to-set-up system of food-waste disposal that belongs as readily in the living room (given an appropriate elegance) as it does in a basement.

The result of her waste-disposal system is a black, crumbly humus that can enhance the beauty of houseplants or boost the productivity of the vegetable bed.

For the past ten years Mary Apelhof has let the worms eat her garbage. The worms in question are a species of earthworm known commonly as the red wriggler, the manure worm, the brandling, among others. In any event, they are the type of worm most commonly sold by worm farms and known to science as *Eisinia foetida.*

As she sees it, these unobtrusive, yet quietly efficient, creatures can do the same thing for all of us. Apparently, the National Science Foundation thinks so, too, for it has awarded to Mrs. Apelhof a $25,000 grant to develop and refine the system further.

Mrs. Apelhof keeps her worms in a simple 1-2-3 box (1 foot deep, 2 feet wide, and 3 feet long), which she says can handle the food waste of a family with 4 to 6 members. In contrast, a friend of hers has a more ornate "worm farm," which also doubles as a window seat in the living room. As a rule of thumb, you should have as many square feet of surface area for your disposal unit as there are pounds of waste produced in a week.

Mrs. Apelhof collects the food waste from her kitchen in a covered pail and once or twice a week buries it in the bedding of the worm bin. She buries it in a different space each week so that 8 or 9 weeks elapse before she returns to the original area. By that time there is barely a trace of the garbage in its original form because most of it has become a rich black compost after passing through the worms' digestive tracts.

There is, she says, almost no smell to a worm farm. The odor that comes with a week's collected garbage quickly disappears once it is buried and the worms get hold of it.

There is a how-to manual on the subject, entitled *Worms Eat My Garbage*, by Mary Apelhof (Flower Press, 10332 Shaver Road, Kalamazoo, MI 49002). In the press release accompanying the book, H. Lewis Batts, Jr., executive director of the Kalamazoo Nature Center, summed up the book neatly when he described it as an "enjoyable, readable, realistically described account of how you can convince earthworms to process your garbage for your benefit."

Kitchen Composter Turns Scraps to Fertilizer

Summer and Winter, the Slurry It Produces Feeds a Garden or a Compost Heap

I once owned a gardening aid called a Kitchen Composter that among other things helped us grow a superabundant crop of cucumbers and other vegetables.

Built along the lines of a kitchen disposal unit, the composter's sole reason for existing was to devour kitchen waste, including chicken bones and peach pits, grinding it into a slurry that made great liquid fertilizer for cukes and anything else that puts down roots.

Those folks whose job it is to gather statistics on the domestic scene suggest that the average family throws away 500 pounds of food waste in the form of carrot scrapings, potato peelings, and table scraps every year. Now that is an impressive volume of plant nutrients.

If processed properly, the food waste has the potential of producing 500 pounds of fresh vegetables in your kitchen garden or an impressive number of pretty flowers, if you prefer.

The trouble with kitchen waste is that it is soft and soggy. Unless mixed with the right proportion of dry materials, it will quickly make a compost heap look unsightly and smell a whole lot worse. Moreover, it can attract everything from starlings to raccoons to your heap. It also tends to gum up standard garden shredders, which are designed to handle dry to only slightly moist materials.

The company that made the Kitchen Composter has gone out of business, but the high-powered Vita-Mix blender, which can pulverize chicken bones and leathery banana skins, is an excellent substitute.

During the growing season I processed our kitchen waste twice a week and then diluted the slurry to the consistency of chicken noodle soup. This mixture was then applied directly to the cucumbers, tomatoes, and broccoli. All responded positively to this "soup," the cucumbers best of all because they received it every week, the others at less frequent intervals.

Never apply undiluted slurry directly around the plants, as it can settle and dry out into a thick leatherlike skin that cuts off the supply of air to the roots. I did that once and suffocated a hill of cukes in the process. From then on I kept rigidly to the souplike slurry. If you do detect a skinlike buildup, simply scratch the surface with a fork.

These finely ground materials are readily consumed by the soil microorganisms and converted into nutrients that the plants take up. You will find that this sort of feeding stimulates and builds up the colonies of bacteria in your soil so that the waste is converted into humus and plant nutrients at an increasing pace.

You develop, in other words, an active, healthy soil, rich in nutrients, that resists impaction, absorbs and retains moisture, and makes for vigorous plant growth.

The slurry also makes a good activator when added to a compost heap. In winter I often spread the slurry on the ground (undiluted at this time of year) and cover it with a little mulch. If the snow is deep, I simply dig a trench above the garden bed and dump in the slurry. When the thaw eventually comes around, the slurry will settle in the soil and rapidly decompose.

I grind up all kitchen waste, including meat scraps but not fat. Meat scraps when ground up and mixed in with other waste do not attract animals and break down ultimately into nitrogen.

An interesting story about the use of kitchen slurries in the garden is told by the Vita-Mix people.

A woman who uses her Vita-Mix to blend up kitchen waste for the garden gave most of each evening's contribution to her roses. The resulting improvement was remarkable, in her words, so much so that certain neighbors became covetous, or so it seemed. In fact, she was certain that a few of her choice blooms were disappearing.

Later, when visiting the Los Angeles County Fair, she found out why. As she strolled through the garden exhibits with her neighbors, they pointed out some prize-winning rose blooms. Closer inspection showed that they bore her name. Her friends, so impressed with the blooms in her garden, had secretly entered them in the fair.

Scattering unground kitchen waste on the surface of the soil would be unsightly, but pureed waste virtually disappears into the soil right away so that it never appears unsightly. More important is the fact that this form of sheet composting has proven to be a most effective way to feed plants.

A word of caution: If you grind waste for the garden on a regular basis, it is probably wise to invest in a second container for the blender.

An Easy Way to Compost?—Try Digging a Ditch

Someone asked me recently if there wasn't a simpler way to make compost.

"Yes," I said, "if you're prepared to dig a ditch."

The inquirer was looking for a system that eliminated the need to turn compost. He didn't want to worry about the wet-dry mix of materials or be concerned over such technicalities as the carbon-nitrogen ratio. He also wanted to eliminate what he termed "unsightly" piles of garbage but didn't want to pay for "gadgets," effective as these might be, in which to make his compost.

What is sometimes known as trash-in-the-trench composting meets these requirements. It is also very effective. I've seen it work in Africa, England, and here in the United States.

Each evening, or whenever suitable, the day's collection of garden residues, such as weeds, lawn clippings, and spent flowers, along with kitchen scraps, are thrown into a ditch and covered with a little soil. Nothing could be simpler. The only real effort involved is the initial digging of the ditch.

Compost Can Be Dug Up

Once filled, the ditch can be used as a bed for planting vegetables or flowers, or the compost can be dug up and spread elsewhere. The compost is rich, though not quite as high in nitrogen as compost made by the more active conventional method. Because there is no marked rise in temperature in trench-made compost, weed seeds and undesirable soil organisms are not necessarily destroyed. However, many are eliminated simply by competition from the billions of beneficial organisms.

I first discovered trench composting eighteen years ago when I climbed a steeply winding path to some gardens high on an African mountainside. There I saw how remarkably fertile soil can become through the use of such mundane materials as grass, weeds, kitchen scraps, and other organic waste.

Method Helped Tribesmen

In Africa I met Robert Mazibuko, who had been hired to show his fellow Zulu tribesmen how to grow vegetables in South Africa's Valley of a Thousand Hills, a beautiful but agriculturally marginal region because of the topography, a heavy wet season, and a four-month dry period.

He succeeded to a remarkable degree by using trench composting. He dug trenches across the slope of the land and filled them with organic matter—anything he could get hold of, including paper. Finally, he added a few inches of soil on top. These became the beds that produced so abundantly. He planted as soon as a bed was complete, without waiting for decomposition.

In my own experience, I find that earthworms by the thousands are quickly attracted to such trenches. Within a matter of weeks, depending on the weather and the warmth of the soil, this waste has decomposed considerably.

Freezing, Thawing Helps

The method also works well in winter. In this instance decomposition is very slow, but the freezing and thawing mechanically breaks down the waste.

One gardener I know digs a trench about 18 inches deep and 2 feet wide down one side of his garden. Each evening the day's collection of waste is thrown into the trench and covered with a little soil. He starts at one end of the trench and gradually works his way along the entire length.

By the time he reaches the end he already has begun removing finished compost for his garden from where he first filled in. Then, like a bridge painter whose job never ends, he starts over again.

In this "easy way" to make compost there is less likelihood of your compost drying out. On the other hand, don't locate your trench in a low-lying area where it may be flooded in a heavy rain.

Fertilizer and Compost from a Plastic Bag

Quite by accident, a gardening friend of mine discovered a very simple way to make very good compost. All you need, he says, is a black plastic bag, some weeds, and the sun. This is how his discovery came about.

After a few hours of weeding one morning he gathered the weeds together and stuffed them into a black plastic bag, intending to put them out for the weekly garbage pickup. Fortunately, he forgot all about it. So the bag lay in a secluded corner of the garden being baked by the sun day after day for about 6 weeks. Finally, it split open to reveal some particularly good-looking compost.

When I examined it, the compost resembled milled sphagnum peat moss, except that I knew it to be far higher in plant nutrients and therefore much more valuable.

Peat moss is the remains of vegetation that has collected and died over the years in damp, swampy regions so acidic that the dead moss never fully decays. Instead, new moss thrives on the nutrients provided by the dead, old moss beneath it. So when peat is finally mined, there are generally few nutrients left, though it's an excellent soil conditioner.

Nutrients Intact

In contrast, the peatlike compost produced in the plastic bag was made from vigorously growing green weeds. Almost all the nutrients that went into their growth remained in that compost. And the fact that the weeds were locked up in a largely airtight bag suggests that few of the more volatile fermentation products escaped into the air.

Of course, composting in black plastic bags is not entirely new. It has been done before, without the help of the sun. In fact, I have heard of one woman who hangs the bags from the rafters of her garage. However, in the case of my friend, it would seem that the sun helped speed up the decomposition.

Now he has more bagged weeds, little compost factories you might call them, out there in the sun. For what it's worth, I'm experimenting along these lines, too. I'm far too intrigued by what I saw to ignore the process.

It might be of worth to add a little kitchen waste to these bags. But I would caution against adding too much to avoid making the mixture too wet. It seems to me that the natural moisture of the green weeds is close to perfect for this type of composting.

If you feel your mixture is too damp, leave the bag open for a day or two to let the excess moisture evaporate. After that, close the bag tight and leave it until you feel the composting is complete. This will be largely anaerobic (without oxygen) decay, a very good process but somewhat odoriferous if disturbed before the composting process is complete.

Simple Appliance Makes Short Work of Fallen Leaves

There is a little tub-shaped machine in my backyard that is doing a lot of work these days turning out an attractive mulch or ingredients for my compost bins.

It stands on three legs at the end of a long electric cord and excites appreciative comment from anyone who happens to see it in operation.

It's called the Leaf Eater, and its appetite for the annual fall crop is nothing short of gluttonous. It is, in fact, the first new concept in leaf shredders to come along in years. It was also, as Bruce Springsteen might put it, "born in the U.S.A."—in Melrose, Massachusetts, to be exact.

But first its limitations: The Leaf Eater is not a general-purpose shredder. It will not handle hedge trimmings, spent roses, or even tomato vines. It was designed exclusively for processing leaves, although it does do a dandy job of converting discarded computer printouts into a fluffy packaging material.

It has been described as an upside-down grass trimmer. More accurately, it is an oversize kitchen blender that uses flexible grass-trimmer filaments rather than fixed blades to flail away at the leaves. Adjustable discharge openings vary from fine (dime-size leaf pieces) to coarse (quarter-size pieces).

It works so easily and simply, and the principle appears so obvious, that the wonder is no one thought of it a whole lot sooner. After all, grass trimmers had been doing a successful job for decades. But Armitron engineers worked on more than a dozen models before the idea of adapting the flexible grass-cutting flails occurred to them.

The concept worked well right from the start, and because it didn't threaten even a careless operator's hand the way a metal blade would, a large top opening is permissable. This makes feeding the leaves into the machine a simple matter. Though it doesn't match my top-of-the-line power shredder in any other respect, it does process leaves more rapidly because of this ease of feeding.

An early problem—a rapidly wearing string—was overcome by introducing a more durable filament. Still more recent is the discovery that by putting two cutting filaments into the machine, string life can be quadrupled.

Damp leaves are processed almost as readily as dry ones, though with very wet leaves the machine must be stopped periodically so that material sticking to the sides of the drum can be wiped off. This takes no more than a second or two.

Not so long ago, an engineering company found that the Leaf Eater could be used to turn old computer printouts into fluffy packaging material for its machine parts. By stacking the print-outs on a table partly straddling the machine, you can feed the leading edge of the paper into the machine. Thereafter the process becomes automatic.

Since the original Leaf Eater was developed several other machines using the same flexible-flail concept have come onto the market. All appear to do an effective job at leaf shredding.

Fertilizer

Soil-Test Kits—Invaluable

I've just learned how Babe Ruth's successor made growing things a whole lot more certain for farmers and gardeners around the country. It's an interesting story.

When the Sultan of Swat left the Red Sox for a greenback-filled future with the New York Yankees, Herbert Atkinson tried to develop some green pastures of his own on the former Ruth estate near Sudbury, Massachusetts. But farming the 400 acres was a lot less rewarding than he had thought. Crop production was, at best, mediocre.

Then one day he poured out his concerns to an old friend, Dr. Carl Draves, an industrial chemist with Du Pont. Dr. Draves suggested that testing the soil, to find out what it lacked, might be a good idea. So together they worked on the project, developing a simple pH, or

acid-alkaline, testing kit that a nontechnical person like Mr. Atkinson could readily use.

It worked well, and shortly thereafter they expanded the kit to detect the nitrogen, phosphorus, and potash needs of soil as well. Before this time soil-testing techniques were too complicated for anyone without laboratory training to undertake.

Striking Results

Armed with newfound knowledge about his soil, farmer Atkinson adjusted his fertilizer needs accordingly. The results were so immediate and obvious that neighboring farmers were quickly driven to ask if they too could have a kit. Mr. Atkinson and his wife responded by making up such kits on the front porch of their home. Demand grew rapidly, and soon farming became secondary to kit making for Mr. Atkinson. Today Sudbury Laboratory, Inc., is the largest United States manufacturer of simplified soil-test kits for the home gardener.

Home gardeners can, in fact, have their soil tested, often without charge, by their local extension agent. But this usually is time-consuming because of the steadily growing number of backyard farmers using the service.

So I bought a garden-size test kit and tried soil testing for myself. It took me just 20 minutes to test two samples, and I now know just what soil amendments the garden will need to make sure of a full freezer come fall.

These soil tests do not indicate what a soil contains in the way of water-soluble plant nutrients, but rather what it lacks. Simple charts indicate just how much nitrogen, phosphorus, and potash (NPK)— or sweetening or acidifying materials—must be added to the soil to make it productive. It's all so very simple.

My tests involved soil taken from a long-established and regularly composted garden and from a proposed garden area that has been covered with sandy subsoil from an excavation site.

How to Read pH

Finding the pH of soil is somewhat like reading a thermometer. Above 7 on the 14-point scale indicates an alkaline condition; below that figure indicates acidity. The neutral point is 7, the stage at which the conditions are exactly in balance.

Plant nutrients in soil that is either too acid or too alkaline are locked up in insoluble form. This means that plants could starve despite the application of fertilizers.

As an example, phosphorus combines with calcium to form an insoluble calcium phosphate when the pH rises above 7.3 and becomes unavailable to a plant's feeding roots. In contrast, when the pH drops to 5 it again locks up, this time with soil iron. While there are some exceptions, most plants feed best between 6 and 7.3 on the scale, from slightly acid to marginally alkaline.

If the soil test shows that, say, 2 pounds of 5-10-10 fertilizer per 100 square feet is needed, you can use either chemical or organic fertilizers with that analysis.

Good Fertilizer—a Mix of Chemicals and Compost

Some years ago I interviewed an official of the world's largest compost plant—VAM, the state-run operation that converts the garbage from fourteen Dutch cities into a much sought-after product.

It was clear, in that meeting, that Pieter J. Houter, head of research, saw no good reason to take either an all-organic or all-chemical approach to plant feeding. "In the Netherlands, we find the two work very well together."

In fact the Dutch, heavy users of chemical fertilizers, also take full advantage of every ounce of plant and animal waste generated in their small but very productive land. Nothing goes to waste.

Ultimately, It's All Chemical

Mr. Houter saw nothing wrong with mixing artificial with natural fertilizers. After all, he pointed out, in its final form, all plant food is chemical, whatever its source. On the other hand, those who eschew natural fertilizers overlook the fact that, in the process of converting to the nutrient solutions plants feed on, these organic substances improve soil structure and boost microflora that contribute so much to the well-being of plants.

For my part, I long used chemical fertilizers in conjunction with compost in my vegetable garden. But for years now, I have not done so, not so much because of any antipathy to artificial fertilizers, but rather because they no longer seem necessary in my heavily composted soils.

But let's look at some of the pros and cons of both artificial and natural fertilizers.

Most artificial fertilizers are highly soluble. For this reason, nutrients are immediately available to the plants. For the same reason, they are not long-lasting. The nitrogen in the fertilizer is readily leached away, and some is lost to the atmosphere in the form of gas. The phosphates and potash are somewhat more stable.

Don't Use Too Much

Use considerable care in applying chemical fertilizer as it will burn any foliage it falls on and will even damage roots if too heavily applied. Many a garden has failed miserably because gardeners, eager for results, have poured on the fertilizer in the belief that if one handful is good, two are better. They aren't.

In recent years, some brands of timed-release fertilizers have come onto the market in an attempt to duplicate one major advantage of organic fertilizers—durability. Concentrated nutrients, encased in a membranelike substance, are slowly released to the plants over several months. One application a season is generally sufficient.

Natural fertilizers—bone meal, leather dust, greensand, compost, to name a few—release nutrients over a long period, sometimes over several years. They are considered safe in that they will not burn plants (except for some hot manures such as chicken, rabbit, and fresh horse manure) however heavy the application. All organic materials improve the water-holding and air-holding capacity of the soil.

Bags Marked

Fertilizers sold commercially must, by law, be marked with the NPK ratio—the percentage of water-soluble nitrogen, phosphate, and potash—it contains.

A typical bag of artificial garden fertilizer might read 5-10-10. That means that 100 pounds of that fertilizer will contain 5 pounds of nitrogen, 10 pounds of phosphate, and 10 pounds of potash. The rest is filler material included to help spread the fertilizer more easily.

Organic fertilizers are similarly rated, but this is somewhat unfair because the NPK test ignores the humus-building value of the remaining material.

Humus improves soil structure. You might say it makes the soil a more comfortable place for a plant to live.

Fireplace Can Cut Fuel Bill—and Fertilize Garden

The oil delivery man scratched his head in disbelief. He even checked to be sure he had come to the right address. He had just filled our tank, and the total cost in these price-inflated days came to only $27. Other homes in the area were taking 3 and 4 times as much, he said.

So it seems our investment in an efficient wood stove is paying off. More than that, it is yielding gardening dividends, too. Even as it radiates cheery warmth into our home, it is manufacturing a much-needed by-product for the soil—wood ash.

That's right, that fluffy gray residue from the fireplace that generally ends up in the town dump is a fertilizer. If it were bagged and sold in the local garden outlet, it would probably carry a 0-2-8 NPK marking. In fact, the ash from broadleaf trees can contain as much as 10% potash; conifer wood ash averages around 6%. Both types contain about 2½% phosphate.

So, wood ash is a valuable plant food. It is also a pretty effective insect repellent. No wonder gardeners who get to know it won't do without it.

An enterprising friend of mine sells firewood to Boston's apartment dwellers during the winter. Part of the deal is that he will clean out the fireplaces each time he makes a new delivery. That's how much he values the ash. Now I'm doing the same thing with the residue from my own fireplace—hoarding it. I have great plans for its use next year.

Potash is essential for the development of sturdy plants and for the production of sugars and starches. Beets, sweet corn, and carrots particularly can benefit from potash. Potatoes love potash, too, but too heavy an application of wood ash could make the soil too sweet for these acid-loving plants.

One regular wood-ash user tells me tomatoes become a rich red color and seem to keep longer after harvest "when I'm liberal with the ashes." Another contends his vegetables "are sweeter and more colorful" because of the wood ash.

On most garden soil, particularly on more acid Eastern soils, spread 5 pounds of wood ash for every 100 square feet of garden. Your sweet corn will appreciate as much as 7½ pounds.

Had any trouble with cutworms? Wood-ash users contend they vanish quickly once the wood ash is spread around. The cabbage worm, bean beetle, cucumber beetle, squash bug, and root maggot all apparently dislike the presence of wood ashes so much that they disappear.

"I doubt if it kills them," one gardener told me, "but they sure don't stay long when wood ash is spread around." This gardener lightly dusts the ash on his plants once a week.

A word of warning: If your soil is already a little on the alkaline side, confine the use of wood ash to such alkaline-loving plants as beets.

It is essential to keep wood ash dry during storage because the potash it contains is very soluble in water. Forget the wood ash that was left out in the rain after the barbecue. It is no longer a fertilizer.

So, when the snows come tumbling down this winter and the north wind howls around the eaves, go ahead and enjoy the cheery warmth of your fireplace. And whatever else you do, save that wood ash.

Put Seaweed in Your Soil for Bigger Harvests

Robert Morse wanted to harvest only the best of crops from his garden. So he took to harvesting a crop from the sea—seaweed. And because it did so much for the fruits and flowers in his own back-yard, he now harvests far more than he could ever use himself so that others may benefit, too.

Every day truckloads of seaweed, the most common types seen clinging to the rocks up and down the Maine coast, arrive at Atlantic Laboratories in Waldoboro, Maine, to be processed into a seaweed powder. The powder is the base for a liquid fertilizer every gardener or farmer can readily make up.

Mr. Morse calls his product Sea Crop, one of a handful of seaweed concentrates now available to home gardeners.

When newly married Bob Morse planted his first garden, he asked a neighbor with better than six decades of gardening experience behind him what made his yard so productive. "Seaweed," was the terse reply. So Mr. Morse went "mossing," as seaweed harvesting is called.

He quickly found what coastal farmers have known for centuries, that seaweed added to the soil boosts production. Research at the Norwegian Seaweed Institute, the Scottish Institute of Seaweed Research, and at Clemson and Rutgers universities here in the United States shows that seaweed benefits plants in many ways. It stimulates growth, improves both taste and keeping qualities of fruits and vegetables, improves soil structure, and stimulates the activity of beneficial soil organisms. Tests also show—though the exact reasons are still to be fully understood—that seaweed checks pests and other problems in crops, increases frost resistance in plants, and revives plants stressed by heat, cold, or thirst.

Seaweed, nourished by the sea, contains some sixty minerals, many of them trace elements, beneficial to plants. But it is not the complete fertilizer, falling short of phosphates. Composting it with chicken or rabbit manure is said to produce an ideal plant food.

While seaweed applied directly to the soil is good, it is as a liquid foliar fertilizer that it is most beneficial. Seaweed extract, in fact, has been found to be 8 times more effective when sprayed on the leaves of growing plants than when applied directly to the soil.

Apply As Spray

It is best to apply the seaweed solution in a fine spray, until enough of the solution has gathered on the leaves so that it begins to run off. Apply the solution preferably in the morning, when plant energy is at its peak, or in the late afternoon. It also helps to add a biodegradable detergent (¼ teaspoon to a gallon) to the solution. As a wetting agent the detergent helps leaves and seeds absorb the solution more freely.

While seaweed concentrate might seem expensive, it is diluted so that a little goes a long way. One small bottle should last an average home an entire season. A spraying once or twice a month is all that is necessary. The solution also can be used to presoak seeds as a rooting solution and when transplanting.

Another advantage of seaweed concentrate is that it can be mixed with any other spray you might wish to use.

Purity Test for Chemical Fertilizers

In the laboratory just in back of his office, Bob Peters, founder of the Peters's fertilizer company, pours room-temperature water into a clear glass beaker and adds the appropriate teaspoonful of fertilizer. A few stirs with a glass rod, and the water turns blue. Within three seconds the fertilizer is fully dissolved. It must dissolve "faster than sugar in hot coffee," or it doesn't meet the Peters standard. Then comes the prime test for all water-soluble fertilizers: I place my hand behind the beaker and look through the blue-colored solution. The outline of my fingers is clearly visible. An hour later the clarity is still the same, and there is no accumulation of undissolved sediment at the bottom. Any sediment that settles out after a "soluble" fertilizer has been standing for some while indicates ingredients "that would not be available to the plant," Peters points out. To get such high solubility, fertilizers must be made of highly refined "technical grade" materials. What results is a product with minimal impurities.

After decades in which farmlands and backyards alike have been overchemicalized, in the view of many, the question of purity with any soil treatment is taking on increasing importance. Organic gardeners and farmers have long avoided anything but natural fertilizers with the contention that chemical fertilizers damage soil life. But there is a small school of thought among some organic farmers that questions this concept. Chemical fertilizers alone are not the problem, these adherents say, but rather the impurities, particularly chlorine, that inevitably accompany the cheaper, dry chemical fertilizers.

Philip Wheeler, of TransNational Agronomy Ltd. in Grand Rapids, Michigan, is one who thinks this way. While he promotes natural farming methods and soil building, he also sees a place for "chemicals of high purity."

Mr. Wheeler's own tests show soil life as well as plants benefiting from judicious applications of high-quality, water-soluble chemical fertilizers. The number of beneficial bacteria feeding on the freely available nutrients jumps dramatically within a day or two of the application, he says. As these bacteria die, they release the nutrients to the plants. In effect, the bacteria have taken a highly soluble chemical product and converted it into a slow-release, natural fertilizer that behaves much like rich compost.

Whatever the soil medium, Peters is a strong believer in the "little-and-often" approach to liquid fertilizing. Feeding a full-strength fertilizer solution every other week (still a common practice) provides a feast-or-famine situation for the plants in his view. "A sudden burst of nutrients," he says, "can sometimes shock a plant."

But the occasional fertilizing approach (strong one week, none another) can work well for plants with a soil rich in organic matter. These soils are so well buffered that plants are protected from the shock of periodic application of soluble nutrients.

Mulching

Mulch: Security Blanket for Your Garden

I've been spreading the word around this past week—the printed word, that is. By that I mean I have taken to using the daily newspaper for the initial layer in my weed-defeating, heat-beating, moisture-conserving, soil-building garden program.

That's right, a good organic mulch does all that and more. And for the city gardener, lacking the almost limitless quantities of spoiled hay available to his country cousin, the daily newspaper is a pretty good mulch substitute.

Mulching, in fact, is the practice invariably carried out in nature of always covering bare soil with grass, leaves, and twigs. And because of the benefits, increasing numbers of gardeners are taking a leaf out of nature's book and doing the same thing in the backyard.

Cuts Evaporation

Mulching makes dry-weather gardening possible because it drastically cuts down on evaporation, keeps summer soil temperatures tolerable to surface roots, smothers weeds that compete for moisture and nutrients, saves time by eliminating the need to cultivate, prevents wind and water erosion, and slowly builds up soil fertility and structure as it decays.

If that's not enough, consider, too, what mulching does in the cooler periods of the year. In the fall it retains soil heat weeks longer than does exposed soil, allowing frost-resistant crops to continue growing apace. It allows for the in-ground storage of hardy root crops all winter long, and, finally, it makes possible the year-round cultivating activity of the earthworm.

Papering the Paths

Currently, I'm laying down newspaper (ten or more pages thick) on the paths between my vegetable beds. Then I cover these with shredded leaves or grass simply because I prefer the look of leaves to paper. On the beds I spread shredded leaves directly on the soil, several inches thick, between the vegetable plants. But should I run short of leaves, I will start with a newspaper layer there, too.

A word of caution: Avoid the glossy colored inserts in your newspaper as their inks may contain lead.

I heard recently of some newcomers to gardening who complained about mulching. It killed their plants, they said. Apparently, they had misread the instructions and covered the plants with mulching materials, thereby smothering them along with the weeds.

Instead, think of a mulch as a blanket—something you pull up around your neck but never over your head. In other words, let the plants grow a little, and then place the mulch several inches thick in between the stems, leaving the leaves above the mulch in the fresh air and sunlight. In contrast, flatten down the weeds and cover them with the mulch.

Just last fall I extended a flower bed by covering the neighboring sod with a layer of newspaper topped by 3 inches of shredded leaves and grass clippings. No grass, not a single blade, poked through the mulch this spring. All we had to do was make holes in the mulch and set out the new plants. That's how effective the mulch is as a weed or a grass killer.

In your search for mulch, don't just stop at leaves. Use hay, lawn clippings, compost, hulls and shells, peat moss, seaweed, pine needles, sawdust, and wood chips.

The more woody items require a good deal of nitrogen as they break down (though they give it all back once the decomposition has taken place). So it might be advisable to give the plants you mulch with such things as sawdust a side dressing of nitrogen fertilizer. Remember, though, only the thin layer of mulch that actually touches the soil takes any nitrogen away from it. In other words, a 6-inch layer of cellulose mulch won't take any more nitrogen from the soil than a 1-inch layer does.

There are some occasions when it is not a good idea to mulch. Cold, damp clay will tend to stay cold, damp, and heavy under a mulch. In this situation, dig the mulching material right into the soil. This will lighten and aerate your soil. Once its texture has improved then go ahead; mulch it by all means.

Let the Sun Shine

I wouldn't mulch too early in spring, either. Let the sun shine down on the soil and warm it, boosting the microbial activity that supports plant life. On the other hand, if your mulching material is good and black, mulch early. Black absorbs heat, and, in this instance, a mulch can help warm the ground.

Be careful, too, when you use green lawn clippings. They make an excellent mulch, but they are so rich in nitrogen that too thick a layer will cause them to build up tremendous heat. Use fresh lawn clippings, by all means, but insulate the plants with a couple of inches of less active mulch around the stems.

Watch Soil Moisture

The best of mulches won't do much for a garden if it dries out. So keep an eye on soil moisture. Don't be misled into thinking the garden is well watered because it looks wet on top. Check by scraping away the top inch of soil to see if the soil is wet underneath. If it's dry, it's time to water. And don't skimp.

Determined Mulching Can Keep Slugs Away

Ever since I discovered—and then wrote about—the many advantages of a thick organic mulch, letters have come in saying, "That sounds great, but what about the slugs?"

What about them? I have been wont to ask. My heavily mulched garden has a few slugs (no gardener is totally free of them) but never enough to reduce the harvest in any noticeable way. Nor have I felt the need to set out bait or any type of trap.

Other avid mulchers I have talked to also contend they are relatively free of the slow-moving but voracious slug. I've often wondered why this should be when others say that the moment they apply mulch all the slugs in the neighborhood move in.

Now I think I know the reason why.

Neutral Soil

An extension agent recently mentioned in a conversation with me that slugs "like an acid environment." Now my soil tests out at neutral on the pH scale. Heavily composted soils invariably test this way. So do permanently mulched garden soils where the mulch has been down long enough, say three years or more, for the decaying action to sweeten the soil. This could be the reason slugs do not take over in the otherwise ideal cool and moist conditions of mulch.

It would seem that newly mulched, acid soils are most vulnerable to slug infestation. Often the second year is the worst as the slug population has had time to build up. After three years the slowly sweetening soils should prove less attractive to the pest. (Slugs are also as commonplace on the toad breakfast menu as eggs are on ours. Glowworms and centipedes, in case you didn't know, also feast on slugs.)

Never a Problem

My soil was neutral before I began a program of almost continuous mulching, so slugs never became a problem. Certainly they are no more numerous than they were before the mulching began. So if slugs are a problem, check your soil. If it tests out acid, add a dusting of lime. Wood ash sprinkled in between the plants would be even better. It sweetens the soil faster than lime and will dehydrate any slug it falls on.

Of course, this approach is most satisfactory in the vegetable beds, where a neutral soil is acceptable. Among acid-loving plants some other steps should be taken such as using any coarse, scratchy material—gravel, sand, or cinders—to discourage slugs. A border of these materials about 18 inches wide around a bed will keep out slugs as the excessive amount of slime they must exude to get across such rough terrain will exhaust them, and they will die.

Fly-screening Barrier

Another effective barrier is fly screening cut into 4-inch strips and buried halfway into the soil to stand upright. See to it that the exposed edge of the screening is ragged. A slug can climb up the screen with ease; it's those sharp spikes at the top that give him all the trouble.

Commercially available poison baits, often in pellet form, are effective. Most contain the chemicals metaldehyde, mesurol, or zectran. Be careful to use only those baits containing metaldehyde around food plants. Those containing the other poisons can be used among the ornamentals.

Slugs feed at night, so place the bait as the sun is going down. Take it up again in the morning as exposed bait quickly loses its effectiveness. Follow the label directions carefully. Once the soil conditions are right and your friendly hopping toad is making the rounds, with maybe a glowworm or two to help, the more drastic and time-consuming measures won't be necessary.

Gardening Techniques

Taking the Spadework Out of Gardening

Daryl Lee is self-employed. He runs a thriving business, which unhappily cuts deeply into the time he has available for gardening.

Even so, what he produced in a 15-by-15-foot garden last season was "remarkable," to quote an admiring neighbor. Tomatoes and peppers were the bumper crops, but carrots, beets, and onions performed pretty well, too.

In fact, Mr. Lee would like to expand his grow-your-own effort next summer. But while he could tend a larger garden, digging out the turf to increase its size is "too time-consuming for me to undertake."

Mulching over Sod

There is an easier way, however. I did it with very satisfying results as many astute gardeners have done for some time now.

I, too, know what it is like to dig sod. So in late 1972 I followed some advice in the *Organic Gardening* magazine and extended my garden the no-dig way.

In the fall I covered the grassy areas where I planned new beds with about 2 to 3 inches of shredded leaves. Whole leaves will do if you can get them to stay in place. So will hay or indeed any mulching material. This mulch effectively killed the grass though it didn't get rid of the tough fibrous roots in the soil; however, this proved no deterrent to plant growth.

Come spring I simply parted the leaves, made a cut with a trowel in the soil, and inserted the plant. Then the soil was pressed firmly around the roots and the leaves brushed back around the stem.

The plants—tomatoes, cabbages, zinnias, and dwarf marigolds—thrived. They grew as vigorously as their sisters in the long-cultivated sections. I have heard of other gardeners being similarly successful with a great variety of plants.

Grass Roots Vanish

The story, of course, doesn't end there. When I cleared the beds this fall my garden fork sank deeply and easily into the soft soil. In just one growing season the grass roots, which can take years to decay if just dug up and placed in a pile, had completely disappeared.

What I suspect happened is this: Earthworms, drawn by the hundreds to the decaying leaves, also fed on the dead grass roots, converting them to rich soil.

Earthworms: I cannot speak too highly of them. Feed them with leaves, grass, and vegetable peelings, and they will work for you all day long—and at night, too. They dig for you, aerate the soil for you, fertilize it for you—all for free!

Is No-Dig Gardening Better?

One of the more beautiful and productive gardens in Great Britain has not been dug, plowed, or otherwise turned over in the past thirty years of continuous cropping.

It is the garden of Arkley Manor on the outskirts of London—8 acres of lawns, flowers, shrubs, vegetables, and orchards, which serve as the showpiece and headquarters of the Good Gardeners Association.

The ultrasimple technique employed is to spread a 1-inch layer of mature compost on the surface of the soil and let the earthworms take it from there. These active little workers, fed by the compost, are the cultivators, the aerators, and the fertilizers of the no-dig garden.

I visited Arkley Manor on a sunny autumn morning, expecting to be shown an experimental corner given over to a no-dig garden. To my considerable surprise Dr. W. E. Shewell-Cooper, founder of the Good Gardeners Association, spread wide his arms to indicate the entire 8-acre expanse and said, "All of it is no-dig cultivation."

Composting in Bins

Knowing of Ruth Stout's famous no-dig Connecticut garden, I had come here expecting a similar approach. The principle is, indeed, the same—the application of a mulch to the surface of the soil. But where Miss Stout used hay, straw, and other largely unrotted organic matter, Dr. Shewell-Cooper applies only thoroughly decomposed and sifted compost to his flower and vegetable beds.

The former approach is known as in-place or sheet composting; the latter involves composting in bins. Indeed, 45 to 50 tons of compost are made each year at Arkley in three slatted compost bins (one heap being built up, one maturing for six months, and one in use).

The compost is applied to a bed and the seeds sown directly in the very fine compost. If young plants are used, these are set out and then the compost placed all around them.

While compost is applied to the annual beds every year at planting time, the perennials are given one initial application. Afterward, compost is replaced only as it thins out enough to expose patches of the original soil.

By applying mature compost, some nutrients are immediately available to the plants, while soil microbes and earthworms readily convert the balance to nutrient-rich humus. The fact that the compost, in its advanced state of decay, is dark brown—sometimes black—in color has a distinct advantage.

It absorbs heat from the sun's rays, warming up the beds more quickly than if left unmulched or if mulched with a light-colored, heat-reflecting straw, for example. This is particularly important at Arkley, where the soil is a cold, yellow clay.

Worms Dig Deep

On the other hand, the action over the years of the deep-burrowing earthworms has converted Arkley Manor clay into a humus-rich soil for some depth. The worms, Dr. Shewell-Cooper points out, do most of their tunneling in the top 6 inches, but they can go as deep as 6 feet. This burrowing improves drainage, boosts aeration, and makes channels for plant roots.

Dr. Shewell-Cooper, who has taught horticulture at several colleges, was once an avid promoter of deep digging. Now his experience at Arkley and prior experiments have convinced him otherwise.

In his book, *Soil, Humus, and Health* (now out of print), Dr. Shewell-Cooper says the following about not digging:

> Earthworms do the tunneling or spading better than the plow; properly composted material put on the surface of the ground will keep the "workers" (bacteria, fungi, and earthworms) happy, ensuring better flavored vegetables; the nondigger aims for quality rather than size and sometimes he gets both; most nondiggers are not out to prove orthodox principles wrong, but to show that they have found a better method.

A No-Dig Garden with the Help of Plastic

Raymond P. Poincelot leads the way out to a garden that hasn't had a spade or fork near it for several years. Some newer parts have never been spaded. Ever. Even so, on this July day here in West Haven, Connecticut, the garden is lush.

Mr. Poincelot, who teaches horticulture and plant-science courses at the University of Plainfield near here, would like to see the end of a time-honored but time-consuming gardening practice—tilling or digging over the soil each year.

Except for a few first-time situations, spading over the soil has no place in the garden whatever, he says: "It's a waste of time and effort, and bad for the soil, as well." Follow a few simple rules, he adds, and "you will never have to dig in your garden again." And you'll almost eliminate the need to weed.

Poincelot has joined the company of Japanese farmer Masanobu Fukuoka, who pioneered the concept near the end of World War II, the late Ruth Stout of Connecticut, and Dr. Shewell-Cooper of England's Arkley Manor in making no-dig gardening a success.

For several years Poincelot had a bed of perennial flowers by his driveway that needed a little extra color. So each year he'd plant a few flowering annuals, poking them in wherever he could find the space. But he couldn't dig over a perennial bed without damaging the established plants. So, using a bulb planter, he'd make a small hole, fertilize it, and pop in a transplant.

To his surprise, he found these flowers did as well as any he planted in the all-annual beds he dug over each year. So Poincelot began experimenting with the no-dig concept and became convinced that while turning the soil may be a part of large-scale farming, it isn't needed in the garden.

Poincelot says that apart from adding to the workload in a garden, digging leads to other problems:

❧ When trodden upon, freshly turned soil will compact to the depth that the soil has been loosened, whereas unbroken soil can withstand the pressure. In agriculture the problem is called *plow-pan*.

❧ Each cubic foot of topsoil is filled with thousands of tiny weed seeds that lie dormant until some disruption, either natural or manmade, brings them to the surface. By turning over the soil, you literally "create your own weed problem," Poincelot says. In his unmulched flower beds he has only to weed occasionally, and he does this with a stirrup hoe that cuts down the weeds just below the surface.

🐛 When soil is loosened, organic matter is exposed to more air, where it readily oxidizes and is lost to the atmosphere. The decomposition of organic matter is necessary to feed plants, but in loose soil the decomposition is often so rapid that many nutrients are gone before the plants can make use of them.

After looking into several mulching options, Poincelot decided on black plastic because of its ability to warm up the soil in the spring, to retain soil moisture, and to suppress weeds. This is how he prepares his garden:

1. Early in the spring he scatters fertilizer and/or compost and manure over the surface of the beds.
2. He covers the beds with black plastic sheets (4 mm thick) and anchors them in place with U pins made from cut-up wire hangers.
3. At planting time, he presses a bulb planter through the plastic into the soil. This makes a perfect planting hole for a transplant from a 10- or 12-ounce polystyrene cup.

Poincelot admits that under certain situations there may be a need for an initial digging of a garden bed, but he says this should be a one-time-only occurrence to clear rocks and large stones; to dig in organic matter to improve air penetration in heavy clay; or to add water-storing capacity to sandy soils.

A patch of lawn is one of the best places to start a no-weed garden, Poincelot says. Simply sprinkle a little manure over the surface and cover the area with black plastic. Within a month, the turf will be totally destroyed—its mass of roots decaying into valuable humus—and ready for planting.

Old French Method Yields Supergarden

I once spent the better part of a day with a soft-spoken young man who arrived at my home bearing a message of hope for a food-short world.

It is possible, he said, "to grow more vegetables than you ever thought possible on less land than you can imagine." What he went on to say sounded fascinating.

He represented Ecology Action of the Midpeninsula, whose research on a few acres of subsoil at a Palo Alto, California, industrial park suggests that vegetable yields several times the national commercial average are possible using what is termed the *biodynamic/French-intensive method* of horticulture.

In the 1890s French-intensive techniques were developed on 2 acres of land outside Paris. Trenches several feet wide were dug and filled with 18 inches of horse manure (then readily available) and covered with a few inches of topsoil.

In such nutrient-rich beds it was possible to grow plants so close together that, when mature, their leaves would just meet. This way the plants themselves formed a living mulch, which kept the soil from drying out quickly and cut down on weed growth. Under such conditions the gardeners reportedly grew many crops a year.

To these intensive, wide-row methods the Ecology Action folk added the biodynamic principles of double digging and raised beds.

After just four seasons of gardening and record keeping, John Jeavons, who gave up a high-paying job as a systems analyst to head up Ecology Action, was convinced that an average family can grow much of its own food using these methods and save a lot of money in the process.

"Our work indicates that a family of four can grow a one-year supply of vegetables and soft fruits (1,300 pounds, according to the United States Department of Agriculture) on 600 square feet of garden," he said, adding that "the work required for this, averaged over the season, would be fifteen minutes per person per day."

All this was possible where the growing season is six months long. A four-month growing season would require a proportionately larger garden or the addition of "simple minigreenhouses."

This is how the system operates: Mark off a bed 4 to 5 feet wide and whatever length is appropriate. Cover the bed with 2 inches of compost or aged manure—less if the soil is already in reasonable shape.

Now, start at one end, dig a trench 1 foot deep and roughly 1 foot wide across the width of the bed. Put the soil you have removed on one side. Next, loosen the soil at the bottom of the trench for approximately 12 inches. (This is more important in heavy soils than in light.)

Fill the trench with the topsoil immediately adjacent to it. In so doing you form another trench. Repeat the process until you come to the end of the bed. Then fill in the final trench with the soil you removed in digging the first trench.

To a bed such as this Jeavons adds 4 pounds of fish meal and 2 pounds of bone meal per 100 square feet.

The addition of compost or manure, plus the loosening of the soil, will automatically raise the beds above the level of the surrounding paths. The benefits of raised-bed planting—loose, aerated soil with good drainage—were apparently first discovered by the Greeks some two thousand years ago.

When Ecology Action took over its garden site in 1972 the topsoil had largely been cleared away. What was left was a heavy, nutrient-deficient clay with 35% rock and construction debris content. It was also very alkaline.

Each year the soil improved so much by these methods that it was not uncommon for yields to double from one year to the next. The soybean crop yield, for example, doubled in one year to double the national average, according to Jeavons. But zucchini was the champion producer of them all. A 6-by-19-foot bed produced 550 pounds of zucchini valued at $250 retail or $125 wholesale. The cost to Ecology Action was $3.80 for the fish and bone meal plus 10 hours of labor, including bed preparation.

A primer on the biodynamic/French-intensive method, *How to Grow More Vegetables* (Ten Speed Press), is available from Bountiful Gardens, 18001 Shafer Ranch Road, Willits, CA 95490-9626.

Microfarming for the Backyard or Forest Clearing

It is midmorning, and already the thermometer has pushed past 90° F when John Jeavons leads the way downhill to the terraced gardens some quarter of a mile away.

I have come to see Ecology Action's new research center and minifarm, developed in the hills surrounding Willits, California, after the organization was forced to give up its original site in

Palo Alto several years ago. The new gardens, green and oasis-like, contrast sharply with the dusty dryness of the surrounding countryside.

The path is precipitous in parts, no place for city shoes. Nor for that matter does the terrain appear remotely suitable for agriculture. Yet its very ruggedness is one reason Jeavons chose the spot. If he can farm successfully on these slopes, where daily temperatures can fluctuate 50° F in a 24-hour period, then it's likely his methods will succeed in most places around the world.

In fact, Jeavons, blue-eyed, tanned, and wiry from years of close association with the soil, is convinced he has an answer, perhaps *the* answer, to world hunger. It lies in his low-technology *microfarming* concept that can turn as little as ⅛ of an acre into a significant food-producing unit.

The microfarm, which would fit neatly into the backyard behind many a United States home, is also designed to settle comfortably alongside an African rondavel, cling to a Haitian mountainside, slip into a forest clearing, or go wherever else in the world a few square yards might be open to the sun and rain. The concept uses soil-enriching techniques so that a small area can produce quantities of food normally associated with much larger acreages. Jeavons calls his approach to farming "biointensive."

Biointensive methods involve raised beds, loosening the soil to a depth of 24 inches, and the liberal use of composts or organic fertilizers. The resulting biologically vigorous soils "have the capacity to produce 2 to 4 times the U.S. [commercial agricultural] average, and sometimes much more, while consuming approximately ¼ the water and 1/100 of the energy per pound of food produced.

Poorer Nations May Benefit Most

In recent years the concept has moved into a number of third-world countries where it is most needed and where its low technology (hand tools, reliance on locally available organic soil conditioners, and manual labor) make it most applicable.

Ecology Action's publications are being used in more than 100 countries, and its principal manual, *How to Grow More Vegetables* (Ten Speed Press), has been translated into four languages. The Peace Corps has taken the French edition to Togo and Benin, and food-raising operations by Jeavons now exist in Mexico, Tanzania, Kenya, Botswana, the Philippines, India, and China, where many of the concepts behind biointensive food raising have existed for thousands of years.

Former United States Secretary of Agriculture Robert Bergland says that Jeavons's approach "has done more to solve poverty and misery and hunger than anything else we've done." He believes that within the next decade agricultural institutions will begin spending a lot of money researching the things "Jeavons has been doing all by himself" for sixteen years.

Perhaps nowhere has the effectiveness of biointensive food raising been more effectively demonstrated than in the little town of Tula, in northern Mexico. The land is hard and dry, and rain comes for only 2 or 3 months of the year. But Gary Stoner, a graduate of the Ecology Action apprenticeship program, has shown that this is no barrier to abundant food production.

Beyond an improved diet, says Mr. Stoner, the gardens have given once-deprived Tula families a sense of well-being, even of wealth. Seeing the benefits in Tula and neighboring La Pressita, Mexican authorities are beginning to expand the biointensive teaching program into several neighboring states, with the goal of introducing the program into all twenty Mexican states.

Jeavons began biointensive gardening in the 1970s on donated land in Stanford, California, and kept meticulous records. "What we found out," he says, "was that the biointensive methods used less water per unit of land than commercial agriculture and less still per pound of food produced."

It takes several years of steady soil improvement before biointensive methods reach peak productive capacity, Jeavons points out. At first, "we got only three-fourths of the U.S. average, or about 3 pounds of dry wheat grain per 100 square feet. But, after seven years, we were at 21 pounds per 100 square feet," he says—5 times the U.S. average. Improved soil also stores water much more efficiently. Over the same period, water consumption fell from 20 gallons per 100 square feet a day during the hottest time of year to just 8 gallons.

Jeavons has found that few agronomists question the yields he gets from biointensive farming. But they do question whether people will want to raise all their food by hand—the "hard way," as they see it. But Jeavons points out that while the bed preparation involves effort and time, it is a relatively simple matter to maintain the garden— 10 minutes a day for a 100-square-foot bed. By most third-world standards the effort involved is minimal.

Hay-Bale Beds Are Fertile Alternative to Stony Ground

After the bulldozers had cleared the trees for a garden site alongside our cottage here, I learned firsthand why New England farmers packed up in droves and headed for the Midwest a century ago.

It wasn't merely the paper-thin layer of topsoil, disappointing as that might be; far more disheartening was the number and size of rocks that lay barely inches apart immediately below the surface.

Digging the first moderate garden bed took the better part of a morning. And with every rock removed, the hay-bale culture of Europe seemed more appealing.

If English commercial growers could plant tomatoes directly into bales of hay indoors on the concrete floors of greenhouses, then surely I could raise them outdoors on stony Maine soil. The no-digging aspect was too appealing to ignore.

Building the hay-bale garden beds was relatively simple, and we were able to have a far larger garden than we would have by simply gardening the conventional way.

The hay bales were a most successful experiment, too—my wife rated it our most productive garden yet. Along with the tomatoes, the cucumbers and the winter and the summer squash produced in amazing quantities, though the potatoes yielded in more moderate quantities.

Some people have made hay gardens by spreading 6 inches of soil on top of the bales before planting them in the conventional way. I adopted the English greenhouse method, in which holes are punched into the bales and then filled with soil.

The method is straightforward:

1. Place the bales side by side and water them until they are thoroughly soaked through. If you can buy spoiled, partly decomposed hay from farmers, so much the better.

2. Liberally sprinkle nitrogen-rich fertilizer or an inch-thick layer of manure on top. This is done to stimulate the decay organisms and get the composting process under way. In fact, using this method you will be making a compost heap and a growing bed at the same time. I used

Nitro, a 10-0-0 fertilizer made from leather tankage on my hay bales. Blood meal or chicken manure would prove equally effective.

3. Using a pry bar or thick, pointed stick, punch planting holes in the bales 3 to 4 inches wide and about 12 inches deep. Place fertilizer in the bottom of the hold and fill it with a rich garden loam. I used Ringer's biological vegetable fertilizer in the hold and topped it with a compost-soil mix. In effect, I made vertical soil columns in the hay bale to support the seedlings until they started drawing nutrients from the decaying hay.

Most experts recommend that 2 to 3 weeks elapse between making the hay-bale bed and planting. This is to give the composting a head start and is the preferred way to go.

I didn't have the time for this luxury, so I sowed the seeds and set out the tomatoes right away, with no noticeable adverse effects. Possibly this was because I used a slow-acting nitrogen fertilizer on the bales. Fresh manure or blood meal might have sparked a more vigorous reaction in the bales, making them too hot for the seedlings during the first 2 to 3 weeks.

Initially, I had to water the hay-bale garden more frequently than the adjacent conventional bed because the hay drained so rapidly. But after about 4 or 5 weeks, the decaying hay absorbed and held water readily. Moreover, by this time some of the roots of the plants had moved into the soil below the hay—soil that remained consistently moist. At the same time, the roots were still able to draw on the nutrients as they leached down from the composting hay.

In any event, during some hot, dry weeks in August it was noticeable that winter squash, planted the conventional way, drooped far sooner than its hay-bale relatives.

This coming season I plan to wrap black plastic around the sides of the hay-bale garden to prevent irrigation or rainwater from wasting away out of the sides of the bales.

In his book *Designing and Maintaining your Edible Landscape* (Metamorphic Press), author Robert Kourick describes his experience with hay-bale gardens in California: "After several seasons the bales wear out but you will find a well-textured soil underneath their loamy remains." He found he could even dig down a foot with his bare hands in this now soft soil.

Which was precisely what I found—except for the rocks, which will keep me with hay-bale culture for some while yet.

Roots on the Rooftop with Shallow-Bed Gardens

In North Fort Myers, Florida, Dr. Martin L. Price is growing kohlrabi, which he sells to a local store. That on its own is of no great significance, until one realizes he is growing the vegetable in a 4-inch layer of old wood chips spread over a slab of concrete.

On the roof covering some nearby rabbit cages, a variety of other vegetables are growing, this time in a thin layer of wood chips and ground corncobs. Elsewhere hundreds of square feet of these shallow-bed gardens have been laid out on plastic sheeting, several of them producing excellent stands of garden peas in 3-inch beds of grass clippings. The purpose of these and a host of other experiments being overseen by Dr. Price is to make it easier for the world, principally the third world, to feed itself.

Dr. Price is the executive director of Echo, Inc. (Educational Concern for Hunger Organization), a technical support group that aids church and other organizations that work on behalf of the world's hungry. The work includes trials in conventional garden beds as well as shallow beds suited to rooftops or other soil-short situations.

Working in this manner, Echo has been able to influence food production in minor and sometimes major ways in over fifty different countries. Echo personnel, however, have found that new growing techniques are not readily accepted in the third world if they have not first been tried in an agriculturally successful part of the world, hence the shallow-bed culture currrently under way at the Echo farm in Florida.

It was the flat concrete rooftop of the Grace Mountain Mission's orphanage in Haiti, typical of many rooftops in tropical areas, that initially inspired the shallow-bed concept. In Dr. Price's eyes it represented 2,500 square feet of prime "arable" land, enough for the orphanage to grow all its own fresh produce. How many other sunlit rooftops, he wondered, could be turned into productive minifarms?

Soil would prove too heavy for most rooftops, so Echo began looking into other growing mediums. Because of a plentiful supply in the group's region, wood chips have been most frequently used. Lawn clippings and ground corncobs have also proved outstanding.

Other possibilities would include sugarcane bagasse, rice hulls, straw, and peat moss. The idea, of course, is to use whatever materials are most readily available and inexpensive.

Initial experiments included beds that were 3 feet deep and others that were a mere 3 inches in depth. To everyone's surprise, the shallow beds produced markedly better crops than the deeper beds. Ever since, experiments have involved shallow-bed culture exclusively, with somewhat deeper beds used only when root crops such as carrots are being grown.

Because the aim is to produce a system that will work in the most underprivileged parts of the third world, the most sophisticated piece of equipment used is the watering can. Plant nutrients are watered in every other day. Straight water is applied on the intervening days.

In the first year all nutrients are provided by hydroponic fertilizers or else manure teas, but in subsequent seasons the decaying wood chips provide many of the nutrients. While wood chips work best once they are partly decayed, grass clippings are a most effective medium within a few weeks.

"We now prefer grass clippings to wood chips," says Dr. Price. "Fresh grass is placed in piles and allowed to heat up. After about a month the grass is placed on plastic sheets [to simulate a rooftop], wet down, and trampled into a rather unappealing mat. Fertilizer is added as though it were bare, poor soil.

"We have been able to plant even small seeds like radishes directly into the clippings if we keep the surface consistently damp until the seeds have germinated. Excellent vegetables are now growing in a layer of grass that has now matted down to only an inch or two thick." After a full season the grass breaks down, according to Dr. Price, "into a rich, black organic soil."

Apart from rooftops, other options for shallow-bed gardens in the United States include paved yards, unused parking lots, and, to a limited degree, on top of soil filled with tree roots. Tree roots need oxygen, however, so too great a shallow-bed covering would damage the trees.

Dr. Price has found that the shallow beds do not use more water than the deeper ones, but they do need watering every single day. The homeowner using the system could not leave for a week of vacation without hiring a "garden-sitter" to attend to this daily chore.

Echo, Inc. (RFD 2, Box 852, North Fort Myers, FL 33903), is a non-profit organization whose *Echo Development Notes* dealing with new growing techniques and underutilized vegetables is sent free to groups helping small farmers overseas. In the United States, $1 per back issue is charged to help defray expenses.

Planting in Broad Rows Uses Garden Space Best

One of the most impressive gardeners I have met in a long time is a Vermonter by the name of Dick Raymond. Although he never finished high school, when it comes to gardening, he communicates as well as a college professor. He simply lets his enthusiasm take over—one reason his lectures on home gardening draw so well.

Mr. Raymond got his early training behind a horse-drawn plow on his father's farm in the days "when you grew your own food or you didn't eat."

He's never stopped growing his family's food since that time. And over the years he has developed some ideas for the home gardener that, frankly, I find exciting.

One of these is his broad-row planting technique. The single row with a wide space in between was designed for large-scale farming, he says. It's far too wasteful a practice for the space-short home gardener to indulge in. The soil, however, must be good and rich for this intensive type of agriculture.

So his rows are broad—3, 4, sometimes 5 feet wide. All low-growing crops such as carrots, beets, peas, dwarf beans, and onions are grown this way in blocks about 4 feet wide by whatever length is necessary. Obviously, if a single row of carrots 20 feet long met your needs last year, a broad row only 5 to 6 feet long would meet those same needs this year.

Mr. Raymond generally selects 4-foot rows because it is easy to reach in 2 feet from either side of the row. "Make the rows just as wide as you feel comfortable with," he tells his students.

In this type of planting Mr. Raymond suggests following the recommendations on the back of the seed packets for spacing the plants in the row but ignoring the between-row suggestions. For instance, he broadcasts his pea seed over the growing bed and spreads them so that they are roughly 5 inches apart.

The idea in this broad-row planting is to have the leaves of the plants just touching when mature. This way they form a protective umbrella over the bed.

This helps in several ways: It keeps the ground cool and moist on hot summer days, saves on watering, and cuts back on weeding because weed seeds can't get going in the shade. It also means a lot more produce can be grown in a given area, which is what good home gardening is all about.

If this approach sounds revolutionary to you, be assured it's a tried and tested one. Dick Raymond has been doing it for decades, the Chinese for millennia.

The testimony I liked best of all came from an elderly couple who attended the Raymond lectures in Burlington: "Why, we get at least twice as much from our garden now," they said.

How to Make Part of Your Garden Grow All Winter

Late autumn is the season when most northern gardens are tidied up and put to bed for the winter. But a few innovative folk are fixing things so that their gardens can stay up and burn the midnight oil, so to speak.

The trick is simply to provide forms of protection that take the bite out of winter for those plants you wish to keep around a little longer or, in some cases, to retain clear through to next spring. This protection can be elaborate, long-lasting, and costly; or simple, cheap, but not so durable.

Wire and Plastic

In my case, I took some tomato cages, unfastened them, pulled the sides out a bit, and placed them lengthwise over beds of vegetables to form arched tunnels. Next, I covered these with clear plastic sheeting, turning them into Quonset hut-type cold frames, or minigreenhouses, if you prefer. Next I placed a rigid pole in the center of the hut to support it in the event of a heavy, wet snowfall.

It was a very simple operation, and it should provide the frost-tender eggplants I covered this way with 4 to 6 weeks of additional growing time. I'm also covering a bed of young carrots (sown in September), so that they will grow rapidly into late fall and more slowly through the winter. I'll also be interested to see how much more mileage I will get out of the broccoli this way.

You may have other ways to extend your gardening season; the variations on the theme should be considerable. One very simple approach is to run a line between two stakes over which the plastic can be thrown to form a sort of see-through tent.

For additional protection, it would help to add a second layer of plastic. Also throwing old rugs or blankets over the plastic once the sun has gone down will help retain more heat.

Be sure the ends of these little greenhouses are closed up at night. On the other hand, it might be wise to open up one end slightly on clear sunny days to prevent its getting too hot under the plastic.

Alton Eliason, who has grown frost-hardy vegetables under simple plastic structures without any artificial heat for years at his Connecticut home, says that the temperature under the plastic can rise into the nineties on clear days when the ambient temperature is only in the teens. "When the sun's heat is trapped inside it can get mighty warm even in winter," he says.

Insulating the Soil

In very cold areas there is danger of frost creeping in from the sides through the soil. The answer, according to New Hampshire grower Leandre Poisson, a solar engineer and dedicated food grower, is to insert a board of rigid foam insulation into the ground all round the structure to a depth of 18 inches. Spreading the insulating material flat over the surface of the ground (like a path) around the structure also proves effective.

On the north side you might cover the ground with bales of hay or bags of leaves, as these will not interfere with the sun. Pile them high enough and you not only insulate the soil but also protect the greenhouse from biting north winds.

Mr. Poisson, who boasts fresh salads all winter long and holds over many other vegetables so that they race ahead the moment spring arrives, has a further trick up his sleeve. He collects excess heat during the day in black-painted cans filled with water. These radiate the heat the moment the sun goes down. According to the Organic Gardening Research Center, a rough guideline is to have 3 gallons of water storage for 1 square foot of glass or clear plastic coverage. If you haven't room for that many gallon cans, include as many as possible. Another option is to fill a can or two with warm water (possibly the children's bath water) and place in the cold frames at night.

❧❦❧

French-Intensive Gardening from a "New" Old Book

I have just taken a fascinating trip back in time—to 1913 and the garden of Monsieur A. Aquitas.

He was, so the records show, "French gardener to A. J. Molyneu, Esq.," of England and a highly regarded one, apparently.

More important, he took time out from his lettuce, melons, and mushrooms to put his thoughts, feelings, and understanding of intensive gardening down on paper. The resulting book, *Intensive Culture of Vegetables on the French System*, shows how large crops can be taken from a small acreage.

Reissued Sixty-five Years Later

The book was first published in London by L. Upcott Gill shortly before World War I shattered the peace of Europe. Presumably, it never made it onto the best-seller list of a nation preoccupied with war, and it subsequently went out of print.

Then a few years ago, Leandre Poisson discovered a faded and fragile copy on a back shelf of a New Hampshire library.

In it, he found techniques—subsequently confirmed in his own trials—whose "time had returned." So he had the book republished by Solar Survival Press. A copy of *Intensive Culture of Vegetables* (now out of print), with markings liberally filling its pages, now resides on my bookshelf.

French-intensive gardening is simply a method of raising vegetables under glass using cloches, cold frames, and similar heat-trapping devices. Unlike heated greenhouses, which try to artificially reproduce a natural growing environment, the French appliances work with nature, assisting it by extending the growing period on both ends of the outdoor season.

Doing the Impossible

In his publisher's note at the beginning of the book, Mr. Poisson states: "The longer and more controlled growing conditions of French-intensive gardening make it possible to grow vegetables and fruits that would otherwise not grow to maturity in short-seasoned, cooler growing areas. It can mean a year-round growing season in the temperate parts of the country. With our recent changes of weather patterns this method of gardening is going to be essential in many areas of the country."

Significantly, too, Mr. Poisson notes that modern building materials and our increased understanding of thermal processes mean that "we can easily improve on the 19-century appliances." Fiberglass and polyethylene plastic sheeting are two such products.

Horse manure—lots of it—was basic to old-time French-intensive gardening. It was used to build up soil quality and also to provide additional heat to the root zone in the early part of the season.

A good hotbed is made by digging a trench 10 inches deep and filling it with a 1-to-1 mixture of old and fresh horse manure. Firm down the manure and spread 4 to 6 inches of soil on top. No advantage is gained by having a thicker layer of manure.

Modern-day gardeners can substitute compost in the warm stage for similar results. In fact, M. Aquitas even suggests that a mild but "lasting heat" can be obtained by mixing manure with leaves.

Containing the Heat

This method is effective even in the open. But French-intensive gardeners go one step further and place cold frames or cloches over the bed to contain the heat generated below and to trap the sun's heat from above.

Even without a hotbed, French-intensive garden appliances speed up the growth rate because they surround the plants with a warm, moisture-laden microclimate. Little "tropical growth chambers," Mr. Poisson calls his cloches.

Remember how a parked car warms up, even in winter, when it is left in the sun? Well that is what happens under the cloches and cold frames. But where the air in a car can be dry, the air in the cloches stays moist, so that temperatures would have to climb above 120°F for the plants to suffer.

Over the years the soil becomes incredibly rich by this method and, according to the author, the grower is able "to set his plants closer so that he can procure three times the quantity of produce in the same amount of space."

Mr. Poisson has been particularly successful with an adaptation of the cloche. Using thin acrylic fiberglass, he constructs a cone with a small air hole at the pointed end. These cones are placed over individual plants or groups of plants. He says they work just as well whether they are 18 inches in diameter (his smallest) or 10 feet wide (his largest). Other gardeners I know have done well by erecting tents of clear polyethylene plastic over their beds.

Several commercially made variations on the same theme now are coming onto the market. Shop around. They should all adapt well to your French-intensive garden.

✦

Raising Plants on a Liquid Diet

Once, to the surprise of several friends and a few interested relatives, I grew a substantial crop of tomatoes and some pretty good-looking carnations without the help of any soil at all. They were grown in boxes filled with sterile, coarse, builder's sand.

The trick, if you can call it that, was to feed the plants a complete nutrient solution—a balanced fertilizer that also included the trace elements, or *micronutrients* as they are sometimes called. Later I grew strawberries of outstanding flavor in pure sawdust using the same feeding method.

Soilless culture, or *hydroponics* (derived from the Greek words meaning "working water"), has gained in popularity among home gardeners in recent years. But it is far from a recent discovery. The English were experimenting with hydroponics 300 years ago; and 2,000 years before that we had the Hanging Gardens of Babylon.

The Hanging Gardens (terraced gardens, in fact) were filled with gravel through which the naturally fertile Euphrates River water was pumped. The plants, if the chroniclers of Nebuchadnezzar II and the Babylonian Empire are to be believed, grew very well in this hydroponic system.

The key to hydroponic success is the complete fertilizer. Most standard garden fertilizers contain those nutrients—nitrogen, phosphorous, and potassium—needed in bulk by the plants but not the several micronutrients taken up by plants in minuscule amounts but which are nonetheless vital to good growth.

In recent years several brands of hydroponic chemical fertilizers have come onto the market to meet the home gardener's needs—Hyponex is one brand, Miracle-gro another.

Automated Systems

Available now are several brands of fully automated hydroponic systems for the home, which virtually eliminate all garden work beyond sowing, harvesting, and the periodic changing of the nutrient solution.

But they are expensive. And if the idea interests you it might be advisable first to experiment a little, as I did, with a few discarded boxes and a bucket or two before investing in such labor-saving equipment.

Fill the boxes with coarse sand, sawdust, or a mixture of both. Drill a drainage hole at one end of the box and tilt it fractionally in that direction. Dampen the sand with plain water, and sow the seeds or set out the plants (if setting out seedlings, first soak the soil and gently wash it from the roots).

Now apply the nutrient solution slowly until the growing medium is soaked. If the nutrient solution is not organic, avoid, if possible, splashing the plants, which might be burned by the salt solution. Now place a bucket or some other receptacle under the drainage hole to catch the solution.

I applied the nutrient solution to the beds in the morning and again each afternoon when I returned from the office. Each morning I added enough water to the drained solution in the bucket to bring it up to the original volume.

A new batch of solution was made up every two weeks, and the old solution that remained would be fed to plants in the conventional garden.

Most of the automated systems irrigate the hydroponic beds from the bottom up. Aqua-Ponics, an Anaheim, California, company, recommends that the timer be set for three irrigations a day—early morning, late morning, and midafternoon. The beauty of these systems, says Mrs. Pamela Taylor of Aqua-Ponics, is that "you don't have to be home to feed the growing plants. The timer does it for you." You can even go away on vacation without needing a "garden-sitter."

In a sense, says Mrs. Taylor, these "hydroponic systems provide 'room service' to the plants—three meals a day are brought right to the roots, which do not need to spread out in search of nutrients." This is one reason planting can be much closer than is generally the case in conventional gardening.

Organic Solutions

Meanwhile, organic solutions made their hydroponic debut in a government-funded, rooftop gardening project in Montreal, Canada, in 1976. Successful crops of lettuce and tomatoes were grown in a sterile mix of perlite and vermiculite using a solution made up of 1½ teaspoons of fish emulsion, 1½ teaspoons of liquid seaweed, and 1 teaspoon of blood meal to each gallon of water. In the Canadian experiments the hydroponically grown crops outproduced the soil-grown control crops. Tomato production was up by one-third.

The Canadians consider this to be a basic solution, which can be amended depending on the needs of individual crops. Cabbage, for instance, benefits from calcium, so the blending of eggshells into the solution would prove beneficial.

Another option would be to use a "tea" made from high-quality compost.

"King-size" Gardens from Postage-Stamp Plots

Up in New Hampshire mobile-home resident Ella May Frazer excitedly tells of the volumes of "good food" she extracts from a minuscule vegetable plot that was formerly a child's sandbox.

Down in Venice, Florida, Ted Olsey does similar things on a 6-by-10-foot plot. And, even if he doesn't say much, the dinners his wife prepares speak volumes for the little garden's productivity. For perhaps nine months of the year, the green beans she serves are probably picked no longer than 10 minutes earlier. Bush squash, tomatoes, and cucumbers are other regulars from that plot.

Thousands of other examples around the country make it plain that a little can still mean a lot in gardening. Put another way, even a postage-stamp garden is worth cultivating. For example, a single tomato plant occupying a 2-foot square corner can yield 20 pounds of vine-ripened fruit—and a whole lot more than that if the soil is rich enough.

A few simple techniques make small-plot gardening worthwhile. Tommy Thompson of Gardens for All, Inc., sums up the approach this way: "Grow up, not out; double up, follow up, and plant in broad rows." In short, employ some logic and common sense.

First of all, common sense dictates that the garden should get at least 6 hours of sun a day. Next, the soil should be improved. Without a rich, soft, light growing medium, the other tricks of the trade won't be worth a dime even in these price-inflated days.

Remove any rocks or large stones. Don't worry about pebbles; they present no real problems and can even do some good in the garden.

Spread the compost about an inch thick over the bed, and top that with a bushel load of rotted manure on a 6-by-10-foot or smaller plot. That should enrich the soil nicely, but for added measure, spread a half pound of bone meal (for extra phosphate) and a half pound of wood ashes (for potash). Now dig all this into the top 6 to 10 inches of soil, and rake smooth.

Your bed should now be raised up a little because of the additional organic matter but also because of the generous quantities of air that can get into the now porous soil. That's good because, along with nutrients and water, roots must have air to live.

Now remember the Thompson advice:

Grow up, not out: Whatever can grow up a pole or fence should be made to do so. Cucumbers will climb, given the chance; otherwise, they will sprawl all over the place. Tomatoes, on the other hand, won't climb on their own, but they can be tied to a stake or confined to a circular cage.

If you want to grow beans, opt for the climbing varieties. They will yield far more for the ground space they take up than the bush types. Grow them up a trellis on the north end of your plot. This way they won't shade lower-growing vegetables in front.

Corn, on its own, takes up too much room for a small garden. On the other hand, you might try planting a double row of this perennial favorite. Let them get started (about 6 to 12 inches tall), and then plant pole beans among them. This way the corn forms a living trellis for the beans. The result is two crops in the space of one.

Double up: The corn with the beans is one example of doubling up. Another is to plant radishes with carrots (mix the seed half and half). The quicker-growing radish will have been harvested before the slower-germinating carrots need all the space.

Interplant lettuce with peppers. It, too, will be pulled and eaten by the time the peppers (or eggplant, if you wish) broaden out. Onions, which will be pulled and eaten as scallions in fresh salads, can be interspersed with a variety of later-maturing vegetables. A little experimenting will soon tell you what does best with what and which varieties appeal to your family's palate the most.

Follow up: To get the most from your plot, plant early in the spring and follow up with a summer crop. Early peas can be followed by carrots; beets can follow spinach; brussels sprouts or broccoli seed-lings might go in as onions grown from sets come out.

You may have other ideas. Check the number of days to maturity listed on the seed packages. If you see there is time to grow a crop before the season ends, then go ahead.

Broad rows: In a small garden don't waste space by planting in single rows with a pathway between each row. Plant in wide rows or blocks at least 2 feet and up to 4 feet wide. If the seed packet suggests planting the vegetable 12 inches apart in the row, then you can safely plant it 12 inches apart every which way.

The idea is to have the leaves of the mature plants just touching one another so that they form a complete canopy over the soil. Onions, bush peas, carrots, lettuce, beets, and cabbages seem particularly suited to this practice. Yields per square foot of garden space can be 3 to 5 times higher than when planted in separated rows.

You might also look into the many midget vegetable varieties that are coming onto the market. They were designed for small gardens and, in many instances, will boost overall weight of produce obtained.

Gardening by the Square Foot

When Mel Bartholomew quit his successful practice as a consulting engineer, he retired to Pheasant Run Farm, overlooking Long Island Sound—and a life of experimental gardening.

The acreage was extensive, and the opportunity for large-scale gardening only a power tiller away. But Mr. Bartholomew chose instead to cultivate a plot small enough to fit far more cramped urban situations. His aim: to promote what he terms "square-foot gardening"—a concept in which the labor needs are calculated in minutes a day, not hours, and yet the garden contributes signifi-cantly to a family's supply of fresh food.

In fact, after initial soil preparation, the only tool required is the hand trowel—year after year.

As Mr. Bartholomew sees it, a 12-by-12-foot plot, or thereabouts, is a suitable garden for most families. "Calculate 4 feet by 4 feet for each family member, plus 2 more for good measure," Mel says.

Significantly, too, all the homeowner need do is cultivate 1 square foot of garden a day by this method. A garden of this size will provide nearly all of a family's salad needs and many of the root crops as well. Once up and growing, the square-foot garden would need to be harvested every day—a few lettuce leaves, some scallions, perhaps, a carrot or two, and maybe some peppers.

"It is important," Mr. Bartholomew says, "to see what has matured each day and to make use of it the same day. That way you get the most out of this type of garden."

What prompted him to design the square-foot concept?

"In helping out and advising community gardeners, I saw that most people, particularly newcomers to the art, overgarden. They plant all the backyard, or the whole packet of seeds, and end up with something they can't manage—or with a large one-time harvest that provides them with far more than they can eat.

"The net result is too many of them get discouraged and quit. So I've designed a system that is manageable, where there's no waste, and which cuts down 80% on the time spent in a normal vegetable garden. Anyone can find time to work 1 square foot of garden a day. They can do more if they like, but 1 square foot is all that is necessary."

This is how the typical square-foot garden might be laid out: First, dig over or rototill the entire plot, incorporating such soil amendments—manure, compost, peat moss, mineral rock, etc.—as you wish. Now mark off the garden into 4-by-4-foot beds with pathways in between. Mr. Bartholomew says he marks off his square plots with 12-inch-wide planks. These serve as the paths so that he never compacts the soil by tramping on it. "Make the paths as wide as is comfortable for you," he advises. "Twelve inches suits me; someone else might want a wider path."

Think of each square foot within these 4-by-4 plots as a separate bed in itself, and plant it to whatever crop you wish. You may want to plant several square feet to the same crop, or you may have 16 separate crops in each 4-by-4 plot.

One square foot of garden space might seem insignificant to you. "Not so," says Mr. Bartholomew, who lists what can be grown in such a confined area: 16 carrots, beets, and onions, all planted 3 inches apart; 9 plants of spinach, leeks, chives, peas, or beans, 4 inches apart; 4 plants of leaf lettuce, Swiss chard, kale or parsley, 6 inches apart; 1 pepper plant, cabbage, or head of lettuce.

When 1 square foot has been harvested, it takes a few seconds for Mr. Bartholomew to prepare the soil and replant it. He simply scatters a little fertilizer over the surface, followed by a trowel of compost (keep up the humus content of the soil at all times, he advises), and digs this in with the hand trowel. Then he sows the seeds of the next crop or transplants seedlings from a flat.

This is how he sums up his plan: "The basic concept of square-foot gardening is to plant vegetables and flowers in square blocks with the plants spaced equal distances in all directions. This eliminates the wasted space between rows. By keeping your planting squares only 4 feet wide, you can reach in from both sides to any plant. You'll save space and you won't be walking on your plant's growing soil, all the while packing it down and preventing oxygen and water from reaching the roots."

Mr. Bartholomew also recommends single-seed planting. This way you'll never need to spend time thinning plants. There is a big saving in seed costs, too. You can keep your seeds viable for years by storing them in sealed jars in the refrigerator, he concludes.

This type of gardening, of course, does not allow for the large crops, the sprawling cucumber or squash vines and large tomatoes. The answer is to grow these vertically in cages or up trellises in areas away from the square-foot garden.

Greenhouses

Helping Your Hothouse Hold onto Its Heat

Increasing numbers of gardeners now snap their fingers at snow-laden skies and go on to produce tomatoes and other fresh-from-the-garden goodies all winter long.

Climate control via simple and relatively inexpensive greenhouses has made this possible, and greenhouse sales have boomed accordingly.

But there is one sour note to this otherwise cheery tune of gardening abundance. Escalating fuel prices have sent greenhouse heating costs right through their often thin and fragile roofs.

Better Materials

If heat-loving plants are to thrive in a greenhouse, the temperature should not fall below 55°F. That presented no cost problem when imported oil was a mere $3 a barrel. But now, oil costs many times that figure. In many northern climates the single highest cost factor in that tomato plant you buy each spring is likely to be heating.

All this doesn't mean you should drop your greenhouse plans or give up on the one you already have. It means simply that you

should buy wisely or take a few steps to improve the heat retention in your existing greenhouse.

Here then are some factors to bear in mind when shopping for a new greenhouse. Just as storm windows help a home in winter, so a double-paned greenhouse with a dead-air space in between is almost twice as effective as one with single panes in retaining heat. In turn, acrylic fiberglass is more effective in this respect than glass. Even thin plastic film is better than straight glass.

A year-long study by Gardenway Laboratories of Charlotte, Vermont, suggests that an 8-by-12-foot, freestanding, electrically heated greenhouse in Southampton, New York, during the winter of 1975–76 would have run up the following heating bills:

Single-pane glass	$299.43
Single-pane acrylic fiberglass (corrugated)	$291.90
Single-layer plastic film	$289.39
Single-pane acrylic fiberglass (flat)	$246.69
Double-layer plastic film	$171.44
Double-pane insulating glass	$161.30
Double-pane acrylic fiberglass (flat)	$128.65

Variables Noted

Vegetable Factory, Inc., of New York City, which commissioned the studies, states that these costs would vary by plus or minus 15%, depending on where the greenhouse was sited.

Most manufacturers now offer double-paned greenhouses. But, if you already own a greenhouse that doesn't quite match up to your hopes or expectations, there are several things you can do to improve the situation.

One suggestion comes from George and Katy Abraham, long-time greenhouse operators in Naples, New York, and authors of the book

Organic Gardening under Glass. They say to attach plastic sheeting to the inside of the greenhouse, leaving a small dead-air space between the sheeting and the exterior glass. Alternatively, rigid fiberglass (more expensive but more permanent) may be used. Or you might use aircap sheeting.

Bubble-Type Plastic

This, say the Abrahams, is "a recent innovation, which is proving very effective." Aircap is the bubble-type plastic wrapping material that has been adapted for greenhouse use by putting an adhesive on one side. Wash the glass wall thoroughly, cautions Mr. Abraham, and "simply apply the aircap to the glass."

Other suggestions: Place aluminum foil on the inside of the base wall to reflect radiant heat that would otherwise be transferred through the wall and lost. Also, plant a windbreak on the north side of the greenhouse. Canadian hemlocks, continually clipped so that they grow into a hedge, are ideal.

Unquestionably, a greenhouse is a worthwhile investment when such intangibles as enjoyment and recreation are involved. But strictly in terms of plant material produced, does a greenhouse pay for itself?

Yes, say representatives of Vegetable Factory, whose freestanding model was tested for a year in the rigorous climate of northern Vermont.

For 12 months, ending in July 1976, Gardenway Laboratories tested an 8-by-12-foot, freestanding model. In that period, the laboratory grew a total of 650 pounds of vegetables valued at $426.23. Operating costs for the year (heat, seeds, fertilizers, sprays, and miscellany) came to $136.00, providing a net savings to the consumer of $290.23, not counting depreciation on the greenhouse itself. (Prices for both vegetables and heating fuel were based on New York City rates.)

Average cost per pound of vegetables produced came to 18.3 cents. Such heavy crops as tomatoes and cucumbers weighed in at 5.3 cents and 5.6 cents per pound, respectively.

Sloping Greenhouse Beats Soaring Winter Costs

At first glance it's the weirdest-looking building—something like an oversize packing crate, one end of which has fallen part way into a Florida sinkhole.

Starting out

All growth in the garden begins with seeds, and the wise gardener keeps a record of everything planted. No need to be fancy; a few identifying notes penciled quickly at sowing time can save a lot of wondering later on.

Future promise

At the right temperatures, seeds can become seedlings in a matter of days. I start mine in individual cells and then pot them up into foam cups (saved from periodic trips to the donut shop). **Top right:** *cabbage seeds.*

Strong roots

A strongly rooted cabbage seedling (top) slips easily from its container. (Foam cups make great containers: Slice down opposite sides of the cup and hold the container together with a rubber band while the seedling grows.)

Nature's tillers

Earthworms (above) are natural tillers of the soil. Dig up a few from your yard, sprinkle them around your newly planted crops, and let the worms aerate and enrich all your garden beds.

Transplants at the ready

A new gardening season gets under way with the first transplants (right).

From the kitchen into the garden— food scraps become slurry.

Kitchen scraps make excellent fertilizer and are often applied directly to my garden beds. First I liquify them in a kitchen blender (top left), converting the scraps into a slurry (top right) that is poured into a shallow trench between rows of plants and then covered with soil (left). Micro-organisms and earthworms quickly convert the slurry into nutrients that plants thrive on.

Sweet carrots

You can harvest high yields of carrots from very little space when they are grown in soft organic soil.

Gourmet leeks

Leeks (inset) also thrive in compost-enriched soil. Their reputation as the "gourmet onion" is reflected in their high price at the supermarket.

Peppers aplenty
Peppers (left), growing in a plastic garbage can and in a wooden half barrel (inset), are edible beauties that also add ornamental value to the garden.

Cuke-laden vines
Crunchy pickling cucumbers may appear to be part of the raised bed, but, like the peppers, the cucumbers are growing in a container.

Caged tomatoes

An easy way to support tomatoes (top) is to grow them in a cage made from fencing wire. Be sure to leave an opening on the shady side of the cage so you can reach in easily and harvest the fruit.

Washbasin turnips

A pleasing harvest of turnips (above) grown indoors in a plastic washbasin.

Bountiful beans

Every vegetable garden should include bush beans (right), in this case a yellow variety. They taste great, yield heavily for the space they take up, and are one of the easiest crops to grow.

The "back forty"

Not always the neatest corner of my yard, but proof positive that compost-enriched soils are highly productive.

Abundant harvest

The proof of the garden is in the harvesting (top). This basket of produce was picked after work one late summer day, and it contains (clockwise) leeks, sweet peppers, globe-shaped zucchini, tomatoes, cherry tomatoes, and carrots.

Tools of the trade (inset).

In fact, it's a different type of greenhouse, a glass-on-the-top-only greenhouse, which inventor Larry Stanhope calls a "sunslope." He patented the idea a couple of decades ago, and the U.S., British, and Canadian governments actually awarded him a patent on a hole in the ground.

The best way to get an understanding of the sunslope might be to take a shallow cardboard box without a lid and cover it with plastic wrap to simulate the glass roof. Now place the box in a wedge-shaped hole in the ground so that the top of the front wall is at ground level. The back half of the box will rest on the mound of sand excavated from the hole.

Of course, the greenhouse should face directly south (or north if you live in the Southern Hemisphere). It's best, too, for the angle of the slope to correspond with the number of degrees of latitude of your area.

Effective Sun Soaker

Now note how effective a sun soaker the box becomes. Though only the roof is transparent, the box is filled with sun all day long except for early morning and late afternoon. Moreover, if the angle is correct the sun will strike the growing area at almost 90°, which is the way to extract the maximum amount of heat from the sun's rays. In other words, the sun strikes the ground in the box at much the same angle as it does in the tropics.

Here's another sunslope advantage: The glass area (sloping roof) is exactly equal to the growing area (sloping ground). That means it requires roughly ⅙ the glass of a freestanding greenhouse of similar floor size, though it absorbs as much or even more heat. Conversely, it retains heat more efficiently after dark because it has only ⅙ the area of greatest heat loss (the glass).

In his Ohio sunslope, Mr. Stanhope's growing beds were formed somewhat like bleacher seats, placed up the sloping ground. He specialized in tomatoes, which he trained up stakes that were set perpendicularly to the sloping roof. This way he could grow the vines close together because the "tropical" angle allowed the sun to shine straight down in between the plants.

"That sort of strategy isn't so important with shorter plants," Mr. Stanhope points out.

There's yet another plus for the sunslope. The right-angled distance between the sloping growing surface and the parallel roof need be no greater than 5 feet. Yet the perpendicular height is such that the gardener can walk perfectly erect.

Mr. Stanhope sees many possible variations on the sunslope theme. Rooftop gardeners, for instance, could erect a sunslope atop a flat roof using the space under the rear of the greenhouse as a storage shed. It might be possible, too, to erect a sunslope on an existing sloping roof.

❧❀❧

Homemade Greenhouse Yields Crops All Winter

When Marge Eliason decides on traditional New England corned beef and cabbage for dinner, even though snow carpets the countryside, she will ask her husband to "go pick me a nice cabbage."

And Alton Eliason, known in these parts principally as a blueberry grower, will stride out to his winter garden and do just that—pull a blue-green firmly headed cabbage. In fact, all winter long the Eliasons eat lettuce, cabbage, carrots, beets, turnips, and other hardy vegetables fresh from their own garden.

He can do this, of course, only with the aid of a greenhouse. But the Eliason greenhouse is a simply constructed one that uses only the sun's rays—no artificial heat at all—to keep out the winter cold.

With food prices hitting a new high almost every time anyone visits the supermarket, the value of year-round vegetable gardening becomes obvious. A few lengths of electrical conduit pipe and some clear plastic sheeting made it all possible for the Eliasons.

What Mr. Eliason did was to bend some lengths of the pipe to form half circles or arches. These he fixed firmly into holes bored into a wooden framework that lay flat on the ground.

These arches were then covered with the clear plastic sheeting. In effect, he had built a tunnel—about 4 feet high and 6 feet across—which now served as a greenhouse.

How can so flimsy a covering be effective in a climate where temperatures drop into the teens most winter nights and occasionally all the way to zero?

The answer lies in the tremendous amount of heat available in the sun's rays even in winter. This heat warms up the soil in the greenhouse during the day and at night the soil stays warm enough to sustain the frost-resistant varieties of vegetables.

"I've known the outside air temperature to be as low as 10° on a sunny day," says Mr. Eliason, "but in the greenhouse it has been around 90°."

On sunny days, when there is little or no wind, Mr. Eliason will open up each end of the greenhouse for ventilation. He's even forgotten to close up at night on one or two occasions. When that has happened, "I've found the plants in the first few feet withered from the cold but the rest have been fine."

There have been times, too, when he has come out in the morning to find the greenhouse covered with ice, but the plants have been fine.

Little wonder then that the Eliasons can say, "We don't freeze many vegetables. We eat fresh out of the garden most of the time."

In fact, the Eliason freezer is pretty well stocked—but only with such things as summer squash, tomatoes, and beans, frost-tender varieties that wouldn't survive even in the greenhouse without artificial heat.

Mr. Eliason does get a little concerned after a few consecutive days of overcast weather "when the stored up heat in the soil may begin to run low." But the plants have always survived because "even when it's overcast there is some warming up each day in the greenhouse."

If ever he felt his plants were really threatened, Mr. Eliason might consider putting a few buckets of boiling water in the greenhouse at night. However, he's never had to resort to that in the two winters he has been growing vegetables this way.

Mr. Eliason's greenhouse is made up of three 20-foot lengths, which give him the opportunity of having three separate greenhouses or, as he did last winter, pushing them together to form one 60-foot tunnel. He sees to it that the greenhouses are always sited each winter so that they get full sun morning and afternoon. "That's important when you have no artificial heat," he says.

He also uses liberal amounts of compost both for the plant nutrients it contains and for the insulating qualities of the organic matter. In other words, the compost slows down the heat loss from the soil at night.

Mr. Eliason has most of the vegetables planted and growing before winter sets in. But when a bed is emptied of one crop, he will reseed it for the next. Last winter he planted Swiss chard around February 1. By the first week in March Mrs. Eliason was serving it up at the dinner table.

Seeds

Don't Throw Out Those Leftover Seeds—Yet

The first year I arrived in Massachusetts I bought a packet of Kentucky Wonder pole beans that contained far more seeds than I could conveniently use in one year. So I used them again the second year and also in the third with excellent results. Then I tried them the fourth season and not a single bean sprouted.

I had learned that there is a limit to the viability of seeds kept under less than perfect conditions.

On the other hand, having been told that parsnip seed was good for one year only, I once emptied half a packet of unused seed onto my compost heap and that year had parsnips coming up with the onions, peas, beets, and even the marigolds.

Throw Away, Buy Again

A majority of regular gardeners throw away last year's seed every spring when the tempting seed catalogs come in. Let's face it, it's fun to order new seed. I know the value in crops returned for the

expenditure on seeds is impressive, but such a throw-away, buy-again attitude is wasteful. Folks who store leftover seed properly contend their annual seed costs are half what they would be if they bought all fresh seed each year.

There's a simple germination test that will help you decide what old seed to keep and what to throw away. But first let's look at some of the more popular vegetables whose seeds generally stay viable for more than a single year in a cool, relatively dry storage area.

Two years: Corn, leeks, onions, spinach, hybrid tomatoes.

Three years: Beans, carrots, peas.

Four years: Beets, chard, mustard, peppers, pumpkins, rutabaga, standard tomatoes.

Five years: Brussels sprouts, broccoli, cabbage, cauliflower, celery, Chinese cabbage, cucumber, kale, kohlrabi, lettuce, melons, radish, squash, turnips.

Test for Viability

Knowing all this, take stock of your leftover seed from last year, and give it a quick test for viability and vigor. Then place your order for new seed.

Take four or five thicknesses of paper toweling, wet them, and wring out the excess water so that the toweling remains moist. On one-half of the flattened toweling place ten of the seeds you wish to test, and fold over the other half of the toweling. Now place the wrapped seeds in a plastic bag to retain the moisture, and set in a warm area.

When the number of days to germination (listed on the seed packet) has elapsed, open up the packet and note how many seeds have sprouted. If seven out of ten seeds have germinated you can reasonably expect 70% germination from the seeds you sow in the garden.

Don't be disappointed with 50% germination. Simply sow your seed twice as thick as is recommended on the packet.

Vitality Important

Remember, vitality of the seed is more important than actual germination percentages. This is measured by the speed with which the seeds sprout. In general, quick-sprouting seed produces more vigorous plants. In other words, discard seed that germinates well but not until long after the normal number of days for germination have elapsed.

How to Keep Old Seed So It Will Grow in the Spring

At a Christmas church fair in our area recently, I came across a bargain in vegetable seeds. Packets that would normally sell from forty cents and up were going for ten cents apiece. So I scooped up half a dozen packages of my favorite varieties and went home well pleased.

Now the question remains: How good will that old seed be come planting time in March and April?

The answer is pretty good—better, anyway, than some garden stores would have you believe. Moreover, there is a pretty effective way to keep leftover seed fairly viable for several years. It comes from Dr. James Harrington of the University of California at Davis. A screw-top jar and some powdered milk will do the trick, he says.

Dr. Harrington, a leading specialist in bulk seed storage, worked out the method at the request of the National Garden Bureau, so that home gardeners might be able to duplicate conditions in commercial seed-storage areas. These are always kept cool and desert dry.

Heat and humidity, according to seed technologists, are the two most destructive elements in seed storage.

A rule of thumb for storing seed, according to a spokesman for the Stokes Seed Company, is this: The degrees of temperature and relative humidity should together number less than 100. Simply, if you can store your seed at around 40°F and 50% relative humidity (total 90), it will stay viable for years.

Here are Dr. Harrington's recommendations:

- ❦ Unfold and lay out a stack of four facial tissues.
- ❦ Place 2 heaping tablespoons of powdered milk on one corner. The milk must be from a freshly opened pouch or box to guarantee freshness.
- ❦ Fold and roll the facial tissue to make a small pouch. Secure with tape or a rubber band. The tissue will prevent the milk from sifting out and will prevent seed packets from touching the moist desiccant.
- ❦ Place the pouch in a widemouthed jar and immediately drop in packets of leftover seeds.
- ❦ Seal the jar tightly, using a rubber ring to exclude moist air.
- ❦ Store the jar in the refrigerator, not in the freezer.
- ❦ Use the seeds as soon as possible. Discard and replace the desiccant once or twice yearly.

Dried milk is hygroscopic and will quickly soak up moisture from the air when you open the bottle. Therefore, be quick about it when you remove seed packets; recap the jar without delay.

Even some short-lived seed varieties such as onion, parsnip, and larkspur remain viable for three years if given this treatment from the moment they are bought. Other vegetable seed lasts for many more years still.

General

Figuring Out How Much Your Garden Will Grow

Early one April I dug the last of the winter holdovers from our garden—carrots, parsnips, beets, and leeks—and closed the book, so to speak, on the season.

It had been a pretty good year, in which the garden had supplied nearly all our vegetable needs. In other words, there was no doubting its value. But pound for pound, I have no idea how much it produced. We simply picked and supped and brought out the kitchen scale only when an occasional record-breaking specimen came along.

Now, however, Dr. Frank Williams of Brigham Young University has done the job for me and everyone else involved in communicating gardening facts to the public. He has opened the books on carefully detailed records involving vegetable plots that ranged from 10-inch pots to 50-by-50-foot plots. The results show clearly the payoff in pounds per square foot that can come from farming the backyard, patio, or window box.

For a Family of Four

For instance, with as little as 54 hours of work and a 50-by-50-foot plot, you can produce 1,900 pounds of vegetables—more than enough to feed a family of four for an entire year. Bear in mind, however, the tests were conducted on good farm soil that had been much improved over many years.

For years this professor of agronomy has tried to convince people of the benefits of gardening, but never before, he says, has he had such persuasive information.

He also ran tests on 5-by-5-, 10-by-10-, 20-by-20-, and 15-by-20-foot gardens as well as gardens in containers to determine the amount of vegetables each can produce, the costs of that production, and the amount of time taken to care for the garden.

Dr. Williams is a member of a team of scientists working through the Ezra Taft Benson Agriculture and Food Institute to help improve food production and the economic status of people throughout the world. The team believes backyard gardening is one way to solve world food shortages and now has statistics to back this view.

Standard Crops Used

Growing standard garden crops—cabbage, lettuce, carrots, peas, beans, tomatoes, summer squash, cucumbers, and, in the larger plots, crops such as potatoes—Dr. Williams found that a 5-by-5-foot garden produced 59 pounds of vegetables, cost $5 in seeds, and involved 2.9 hours of work. The 10-by-10-foot garden produced 184 pounds of vegetables, cost $5.25, and involved 5 hours of work. The 20-by-20-foot plot produced 485 pounds of vegetables, cost $6.30, and involved 15.7 hours of work; the 15-by-20-foot garden produced 403.5 pounds of vegetables for $12.05 and involved 16.1 hours of work.

You can lower costs by 20% or more the next year by storing left-over seeds, according to Professor Williams.

Most of the work in the gardens involved planting and weeding and was done by inexperienced gardeners. On the other hand, the planning, an important phase of successful gardening, was done by agronomists.

Apartment Gardens

Because even apartment dwellers may want to grow some of their own food, Dr. Williams ran tests in containers. He found that a 10-inch pot can yield 2.8 pounds of tomatoes in 58 days, 2.32 pounds of cabbage in 58 days, 0.29 pound of carrots in 42 days, 0.79 pound of Swiss chard in 42 days, or 2.3 pounds of zucchini in 58 days.

A box 60 inches by 21 inches and 11 inches deep produced 5.45 pounds of pole beans, Swiss chard, peas, cabbage, parsley, and tomatoes in just 2 months.

With the cost of vegetables likely to continue rising each year, every pound of home-produced food will help.

But, says Dr. Williams: "Gardening and home production has a value beyond the money which can be made and saved. Perhaps the greatest value is the feeling of competence that comes from knowing it can be done."

Making the Most of Your Produce

A well-harvested garden can help you hold down food costs the year round. But you lose that advantage quickly if you don't make the most of what you have when your garden is producing heavily. An onrush of tomatoes or a deluge of zucchini is a harvesting opportunity, not an embarrassing glut to be gotten rid of.

By late July one season, for example, Pauline Baker's Burlington, Vermont, garden was producing more fresh tomatoes than her family could eat. So she decided to sell some of the surplus.

The best she could get for her fresh produce, however, was twenty-six cents a pound—roughly one-third the going retail price.

"They're worth more to me as spaghetti sauce," she reasoned and promptly began processing the excess.

Then, Mrs. Baker says, is when she learned that, to get the most out of a garden, canning or freezing should be a season-long program—taking place whenever the garden is producing more than can be eaten immediately.

Tiresomeness Avoided

By doing small batches at a time, processing never became a tiresome chore. And by the time the first frosts had blackened the vines two months later, she had frozen seventy quarts of spaghetti sauce, twenty small jars of tomato paste, and four gallons of juice. She canned or froze a variety of other vegetables, including zucchini, which went into a relish for which she is renowned.

Canning and preserving need not burden the family's chief cook. Other family members who have food specialties can join in. Perhaps someone has a favorite tomato sauce recipe. Let him process the tomatoes for that. Perhaps a son or daughter likes dill pickles. Then let the youngsters put up some of the cucumbers. In this way, what might become a burdensome chore if imposed entirely on one person can be an occasion for family fun.

There are other ways, too, of stretching gardening profits and pleasure. Vigorous harvesting of certain vegetables is one strategy. Then there is double, and even triple, cropping—where more than one crop is taken from a given area in a season.

Early Harvest Encourages Growth

One piece of advice from a veteran Vermont gardener has served me well. "Remember," he said, "it is nature's intention that a plant should produce seed, so the more you harvest before the seed is mature, the more the plant will go on producing."

Summer squash is a case in point. For best results, he says, pick them when the young squash is no thicker than 1 to 2 inches in diameter. He has similar advice for cucumbers. "Pick them when they're about 4 inches long," he says. "You get both quantity and quality that way." Tests have proved this over and over again, he adds.

The effect is similar with snow peas, where the whole pod is picked and eaten before the peas develop. Some gardeners insist that there also is a marginal increase in crop quantity if standard peas and beans are picked "a little on the young side."

You will also get "incredible mileage" from Swiss or ruby chard by ruthless harvesting. Don't just harvest the outer leaves of these vegetables, cut down the entire plant to about an inch above the ground. It will grow up again from the center. By the time you've come to the end of the row, the first plants should be up and ready to harvest again.

Several Crops Possible

In warmer regions, getting more than one crop of vegetables a year from a garden is relatively simple. Peas, which even in the colder north may be planted as soon as the soil can be worked, are generally all harvested by the end of June or early July. Beans or carrots for fall harvesting can follow the peas. Onions grown from sets mature quickly. I frequently follow these with carrots to be left for wintering over in the ground.

Seed packets list the number of days to maturity of a particular vegetable. Check with your county agricultural agent as to when the first fall frosts are likely to occur. If you still have time to reap a harvest, then go ahead and plant. Sometimes it is worth taking a chance on fall frosts arriving late. On the other hand, such hardy plants as peas, cabbage, or lettuce can stand light frosts and so may be planted quite late in the season.

One final hint: Never waste space on radishes alone. When you sow early carrots and beets, sprinkle radish seeds in the row, too. The radishes spring up quickly, and as you harvest them a few weeks later, you automatically cultivate your carrots.

How a Diary Helps to Plan Your Garden

A Detailed Record This Year Will Be Invaluable Next Season

We ate the last of our crop of brussels sprouts the other day. They were as sweet to the taste as usual, but they came to an end far sooner than was necessary. In other years, the freezer has contained enough to keep us going at least into late spring.

It was all my fault. Had I made use of a simple gardening calendar we would have had—who knows—perhaps twice as many sprouts.

Last year I let the optimum sowing time for fall sprouts slip by unnoticed until it was several weeks past. The result of this late planting was that I had to pinch out the tops of the plants (to encourage sprout development) while they were still fairly small. I calculate that I lost at least 4 inches of sprout-producing stem from each plant because of that late start. That's about one lost serving per plant.

Now I'm not about to let that happen again. So, clearly marked on my gardening calendar under June 17 is "Sow sprouts, broccoli, cabbage, cauliflower for fall harvest." A July 20 entry reminds me to sow carrots for fall and winter, and another in September suggests I try more carrots "if there's room in the garden."

An October entry says to erect an enclosure for the coming deluge of leaves; one in November reminds me to take in a bucket of compost (for February seedlings) before the pile freezes (another of last year's goofs). And so it goes throughout the year. I rely on past experiences to make current entries.

In some of the warmer zones to the south, plantings are done earlier in the spring and later in the fall than I would up here. The point is: Whatever planting dates are best for your climate should be noted on a calendar or in a diary that you refer to at least once a week.

Growing good vegetables and flowers becomes easier by the year, and it can be made easier still if detailed records and reminders are kept.

Recently, my wife and I sat down and listed all the vegetables we wanted from the garden this coming year.

For what it is worth, our garden will contain leeks, onions, carrots, parsnips, beets, cabbage, cauliflower, broccoli, brussels sprouts, kohlrabi, potatoes, lettuce, beans, tomatoes, peppers, winter and summer squash, and cucumbers. One possible newcomer to our garden this year is vegetable soybeans. That should be more than enough to keep me busy all season long. It will also keep our dinner plates filled with a variety of good-tasting items clear through to the following spring.

I've marked down the expected planting dates for every one of these vegetables in the diary. Some get mentioned frequently. Buttercrunch lettuce, for instance, gets a notation every two weeks from early April into September. The idea is to sow little and often with this vegetable.

In your garden diary, mark down such facts as how much fertilizer you used, how and when you mulched, what the weather was like, and finally the harvest. This way you will have a complete record on which to base next year's garden plan.

The point is: Put it all down. Don't rely on memory. It's simply amazing how, say, a coming business trip or a family wedding can blow such things as fall carrot planting clean out of mind.

With Notes in Hand, Plan Next Year's Garden

It was raining the other afternoon—a typical nor'easter, the weatherman said. So I put on a slicker and went outside.

The garden can be a pleasant place even in the rain. And while it was too wet to work in, it was dry enough to walk in—to take stock of things and begin planning for next year.

That's right, even while fall's parade of color marches across the land, it's best to start preparing for next year. Ask yourself, What changes should I make when spring rolls round again? What vegetables and flowers should I concentrate on? Should I cut back on some, increase others? What went right and what went wrong in the garden this year and why?

Come to some conclusions, and make the necessary decisions now, while this year's growing season is still fresh in your mind. It's important, too, to get these thoughts and ideas down on paper right away—before long weeks of snow shoveling blurs your memory.

Let the draftsman in you come out. Spend an evening designing your garden. It will be time well spent.

Take a piece of paper and lightly mark it off in ¼-, ½-, or even 1-inch squares. Let each square represent a square foot of gardening space and then draw in where you plan to grow what.

The end result will be a readily managed and orderly garden. There will be no waste of time wondering where to plant what when spring comes around and no waste of garden space either. Plan, too, which crop will follow what. When the early peas are pulled, do you want beans, beets, or maybe leeks to follow? Whatever you decide, put it down on your master plan.

Six to Eight Hours of Sun

Mark on your garden plan the sunniest and shadiest spots. Ideally, a good garden site will have sun from sunrise to sunset. But most plants can get by on 6 to 8 hours of direct sunlight. Leafy vegetables such as cabbage, chard, and lettuce can get by on less. Dr. Edmond L. Marotte at the University of Connecticut College of Agriculture cites this rule of thumb: "If grass grows well in the shady area, then leafy vegetables will probably do well, too."

Meanwhile, I'm making use of a packet of seed left over from spring. It's winter rye, and wherever a space appears in the garden after harvesting, I plant the rye. It will grow in the cooler weeks ahead, stabilize the soil during the long, wet winter, and in the spring can be turned in to add more organic matter to the soil.

Friendly Toads Feast on Pests

I called him Paddy when he made his home with us last season. Now he or his identical twin has returned this season, much to my delight.

As toads go, he's a handsome fellow. But it's not his looks but rather his remarkable eating habits that impress so much. You see, Paddy is a glutton. From late spring to early fall he consumes between 15,000 and 16,000 insects—an all-protein diet that is made up largely of cutworms, potato beetles, chinch bugs, mosquitoes, and a variety of other undesirables.

He's one of an army of garden residents that helps keep the backyard plot in balance and satisfactorily productive. If Paddy is the colonel, then the ladybugs, lacewings, assassin bugs, wasps, praying mantises, and spiders are the troops of this backyard brigade.

Moving Food Preferred

The American toad, like his French, English, and Australian counterparts, has one rule that he insists upon when dining. The dinner, whatever it is, must hop, crawl, jump, fly, or otherwise move around before he takes a bite. Be it ever so tasty, the toad will ignore the lifeless carcass at his feet.

During the day the toad rests in deep shade or under appropriately thick garden mulch and comes out with sharpened appetite in late afternoon and early evening to hunt up a meal. He can be encouraged to stay around if he has this sort of cover and if you wet down the shrubbery on hot days. When a toad is thirsty he needs a drink like everyone else. But like few other creatures, he drinks through his skin by absorbing dew or rain off wet leaves. It will also help if you place a shallow pan of water in deep shade, which he can jump into when he wants to slake his thirst.

Potato Patch Hideaway

Last year the favorite resting area for my amphibian friend was the potato patch where both shade and a deep, shredded leaf mulch existed. His presence may be one reason I had no cutworm problems in that patch.

With the approach of winter, the toad hibernates by digging a hole with his back legs and covering himself up. He must dig below the frost line to survive. Last winter our resident toad made his winter home in a pile of shredded leaves. I know that because I uncovered him in the early spring when I removed some of the leaves to make an early batch of compost. I promptly covered him up again.

In any event, I plan to have an appropriately sited pile of mulch available for him this coming winter. He's welcome to have his relatives move in, too.

In controlling insect pests, don't overlook the effectiveness of your thumb and forefinger. It's remarkable how effective this manual control can be. Each day search out possible pests.

Telling Friend from Foe

I find most pests are sluggish and readily caught first thing in the morning. But know how to distinguish between your predator (good) insects and your leaf-eating (undesirable) insects.

Once in an overhasty attack on some Mexican bean beetles I also crushed a ladybug. I mourned the loss of the great ally all day long. Get a good book—there are several on the market—that will help you differentiate between the goodies and the baddies.

Also keep an insect log. During the coming gardening season note down what time of year a pest puts in an appearance. As most insects turn up in the garden at roughly the same time year after year, such a record will help you stay ahead of a problem by alerting you in time to deal with pests before their numbers proliferate.

Organic Methods

If something gets out of whack and a heavy pest infestation occurs, you will have to do something drastic. This will probably require the use of sprays, most of which are just as harmful to the beneficial insects. This invariably throws the system still further out of kilter.

An organic method that does not do this and that many gardeners have found effective (though the scientific reason has still to be uncovered) is this: Catch a cupful of the pest insects and blend them up with a quart of water and strain. Now spray the strained solution over the affected areas. This may only chase the pests away rather than destroy them, but it does save the harvest. Such sprays also have little effect on other insects.

Another effective natural insecticide is Thuricide—a fungus that attacks all leaf-chewing worms.

Bats Battle Bugs

A few years ago, Merlin D. Tuttle, a professor at the University of Texas and founder of Bat Conservation International, approached a Tennessee farmer with a request: Might he investigate a cave on the farm that housed a bat colony?

"Sure," the farmer replied, "and if you can find a way to get rid of them while you're there, go ahead."

Hours later, Dr. Tuttle emerged from the cave with a handful of insect wings. Dumping them in front of the farmer he asked: "Know what these are?" "I'll say I do," the farmer replied. "They're Colorado potato beetles. They can do a number on a potato field! Where'd you get 'em?"

When told that the wings came from the cave and that potato beetles obviously were a major part of that particular colony's diet, the farmer's attitude toward bats did an about-face. Given a rough assessment of the beetle wings still back in the cave and the approximate size of the bat colony, the farmer did some quick calculations. "I reckon each bat is worth about $5 to me [in reduced crop losses]," he told Tuttle.

To Tuttle and his colleagues at Bat Conservation International, this represents a small victory in the ongoing and often frustrating campaign to get people to recognize the value of bats and to prevent the extinction of bat species that is taking place worldwide. "Last year two bat species became extinct on the island of Guam alone," says Tuttle. "We are losing entire species even before they make it onto the endangered species list."

Loss of summer roosting sites (hollow trees, suitable rock over-hangs, etc.) and the spread of urban centers is partly responsible. But two other factors, particularly in the United States, are a widespread public fear of bats, built up by totally false stories in popular magazines, and misleading advertising by pest exterminators.

But apart from potato farmers, who else would benefit from having bats in the neighborhood? We all would. For one thing, bats will do more to make the evening barbecue mosquito-free than any other wild creature. And they can do great things for the garden, too.

With its incredible sonar system, the bat easily detects and avoids objects in its path, including thin wires, even when blindfolded during scientific tests. For this reason, scientists dismiss stories of bats becoming entangled in human hair and "old wives' tales."

What do attract bats and bring them flying near people on a warm summer evening are insects, particularly mosquitoes. The mosquito senses the warm-blooded human presence and zeros in. In turn, the bat picks up the mosquito's presence and flies close by, and it's likely that the human being has been spared one more mosquito bite, says Tuttle.

There is also a fear that bats are more likely to become rabid than any other animal. This is not the case, Tuttle points out. More-over, the bat that does become rabid quickly becomes immobile and dies, making it far less of a threat in this respect. Bats do not fly out and attack people. On the other hand, if you push a probing hand into a darkened area and disturb a sleeping bat, it is very likely to bite.

Moths are another major item in the bat diet, and the fact that both cutworms and the peachtree borer are the offspring of night-flying moths indicates why the presence of bats is so valuable to the gardener. An occupied bat house, where guano drops conveniently to the ground below, is another plus. Bat guano is a remarkably rich fertilizer. Like penguin guano, it sells for as much as $30 a pound . . . when it can be had, that is.

Building Your Bats a House of Their Own

Plagued by bats? Dr. Tuttle suggests exclusion as a safe, simple alternative to extermination, which involves highly toxic chemicals. The experience of some St. Louis wildlife enthusiasts is a case in point.

This group had no misconceptions about bats, but when they arrived at their wilderness preserve one spring to find that a colony had taken over their cook house, they decided something had to be done. How they solved the problem made a significant contribution to the save-the-bats campaign: They built a bat house that proved acceptable to the Little Brown Bat, something considered no easy task. Then one evening, after the bats had flown off, the members of the group caulked up or otherwise blocked every chink and crack in the cook house that might allow the bats to get back in.

When the bats returned at dawn to find every entrance blocked, they had to look elsewhere for shelter. The nearby "Bat Towers" complex proved inviting enough, and they moved in. A few weeks later, wildlife expert Dr. Richard LaVal examined the bat house and found seventy sleeping bats. There was room, he said, for several hundred more.

Now, the Missouri Department of Conservation and the Washington-based magazine *Defenders*, which broke the bat house success story in 1985, are providing plans for the St. Louis group's bat house free to anyone who might like to build one.

How did the St. Louis conservationists design a shelter that proved attractive to bats? They started by reading up on everything they could find about bat roosting sites. They found that bats are attracted to small nooks and crannies where they can crawl in, hang upside down, and go to sleep. So they came up with a roof-type structure, designed to shelter the bats from the weather, with special sleeping quarters (a series of parallel slats) inside. The slats were made from vertical rows of cedar shingles spaced at various intervals to give the bats a choice of sleeping crevices ranging from ½ inch to 1½ inches wide. The bats crawl through the narrow opening of their preference, cling to the rough cedar sides, and go to sleep.

The key to bat acceptance is the slat structure inside. How decorative or plain the protective roof is of no consequence to the bats. (The plans put out by the Missouri Department of Conservation, however, call for a bat house that would look handsome in any garden. It includes a sloping, shingled roof complete with cupola and weathervane.)

Some bat species live permanently in caves, others hibernate through the winter in distant caves and emerge in the spring to fan out in search of food. Once in their preferred "hunting grounds," the latter species search around for appropriate roosting sites where they also raise their young—one a year. These roosting sites sometimes include barns and attics. Because even the largest bat species can crawl through an opening less than ¾ of an inch wide, they can readily enter many older buildings.

If you plan to build a bat house for yourself, David Robinson of the National Geographic Society suggests doing so in the summer or winter, and waiting until early spring to set it up, just before the bats fan out in search of roosting sites. If few bats have been sighted in our area, you may have to wait for some time, several years perhaps, before any locate your structure. On the other hand, if bats currently roost in a building on your property, they may soon take over your bat house if you erect it near the building they use and then caulk over or block up all possible openings in that building.

The best time to block these entrances is during the winter, when bats hibernate elsewhere. Otherwise, block them up any time after dark when the bats are out flying. Don't do this during June and July, Dr. Tuttle cautions, or you will separate the mothers from their flightless babies inside.

How to Start Seeds Indoors—and Save

A thrifty gardener can parlay a few dimes' worth of seeds into many dollars worth of vegetables. But you handicap yourself from the start if you buy tomato, pepper, or other plants from commercial growers. It is cheaper by far to start such plants from seed yourself—a late winter indoor project that is simpler than you may think.

I never was particularly good at starting seeds indoors, either. Then someone told me to use plastic bags, and the seeds have been sprouting faster and more evenly ever since.

Get a Jump on Spring

Admittedly, folks who live in more benign climates with lengthy growing seasons won't feel any great need to practice this art. But most gardeners in the United States have to get a jump on spring.

Frost-tender vegetables such as tomatoes and peppers must be started indoors to guarantee a harvest before the first frosts of fall. Even many of the hardier vegetables benefit from the extra-early start. Onions, slow growers that they are, are an example. And in New England, cabbage begun indoors can mean cabbage on the table before the heat of summer begins.

Start your seeds in a flat in a soft, porous soil. A mixture of garden soil and some milled sphagnum moss makes a good nursing medium for the young plants. Potting soil will do equally well.

Sterilizing Soil

I've never bothered to sterilize this soil, but some growers recommend it. To do this, put your soil in a dish and bake it in an oven at 250°F for 20 to 30 minutes. Mix in a light dusting of balanced fertilizer.

Now plant the seeds at the depth recommended on the package. Otherwise, a general rule to follow is to plant the seed at a depth 4 times its diameter. This applies to direct outdoor planting as well.

Water generously, and place the flat in a plastic bag (last week's bread wrapper will do). Tie the end, and place in a warm spot, but not in the hot sun. I place mine on the floor near our basement furnace.

Though seedlings can grow in much cooler temperatures, most seeds need 70°F and higher if they are to germinate well. Following this procedure, I've found seeds that previously took 1 to 2 weeks to begin sprouting were poking up in 4 to 6 days.

After Sprouting

After the seeds have sprouted, place the flat in a sunny window or under lights. For the first day, I leave on the plastic package with the end open. After that, I remove the bag altogether.

From now on, keep the soil moist, but, please, don't drown the seedlings. While young roots need moisture, they also need air.

Plants growing indoors frequently become leggy, whereas the gardener would like stocky, sturdy plants to set out. In my experience, leggy plants quickly become sturdy once they have been planted outdoors, so I've never been overconcerned. However, there is a way of growing sturdy plants indoors, too—shake them.

Dr. Cary Mitchell, a Purdue University professor, discovered this when pondering the problem of twenty-first-century space farms. He discovered that gentle shaking or stroking of plants stunts their growth, resulting in sturdier, greener plants. And what may make fresh food available for space colonists in the future has applications here on earth right now.

Natural Stress Apparent

Wind and rain provide the most obvious mechanical stresses on outdoor plants. So in trying to mimic these stresses, Dr. Mitchell subjected herbaceous plants—tomatoes, marigolds, chrysanthemums, peas, and beans among others—to gentle vibration.

The results of just 20 seconds a day of this shaking proved significant over several weeks. "The general responses to stress," says Dr. Mitchell, "is a reduction in growth seen in shortened internodes, increased lateral development, deep greening of the tissues, and reduced leaf surface area."

Besides vibration, Dr. Mitchell discovered that dwarfing is also induced by touch. Simply stroke the plants with the hand, or a feather, or any soft, nonabrasive material. He suggests 30 seconds of stroking (caressing might be the better term) once or twice a day.

Start transplanting when the seedlings are 2 to 3 inches tall. Remember, tomatoes can be planted deeply, but all other plants, as a general rule, should never be replanted more than ½ inch deeper than previously. This transplanting seems to encourage development of a strong root system in preference to growth of the rest of the plant.

One final step: Harden the young plants before you set them out in the garden. For about a week, put them outdoors in partial shade for a few hours each day, making sure they are protected from winds.

Plant Protection

If you haven't time for this sort of operation, you might do as I did with my tomatoes last year. I set the young plants out in the garden and covered them with gallon plastic milk containers with holes cut out of the bottom.

The containers protected the plants from the burning effects of the wind and, because the plastic was not completely transparent, from the full intensity of the sun. Cold night temperatures were always less severe under the containers—though the screw tops were left off night and day to ensure a supply of fresh air.

Keep each container in place by tying it to a stick pushed just a few inches into the soil. In this way, you have an inexpensive cold frame in which to start your own plants, and you get the jump on the economy as well as on the weather.

Crops

Beans—One of the Easiest and Most Productive Crops

When I was in grade school and everyone was trying to do his patriotic best in some rather unsettling times, we youngsters were told that we too could help thwart Hitler. We could, for instance, cultivate a few vegetables at home.

So I elected to grow beans—tasty, nutritious scarlet runners, which subsequently earned me a certificate of merit from the schoolteacher assigned to inspect such backyard efforts.

Nothing succeeds like success, they say, and I've been growing beans ever since.

In fact, beans are one of the easiest crops to grow and one of the most productive. Heavy yields come from even very small garden plots. A 5-by-5-foot bed last year yielded many meals for us with several quarts left over for freezing.

From Ancient Times

Beans in many forms have been around for a long time, as the Greco-Roman origin of their botanical name, *Phaseolus*, suggests. On this

side of the Atlantic the Indians were cultivating beans long before the Pilgrims arrived. And, to his surprise, Columbus found beans in Cuba, which he described in his diary as "very different from those grown in Spain."

Of all the many varieties of beans, the most popular in the home garden is the green, or snap, bean, grown on compact bushes or high-climbing vines.

Beans grow well in average, well-drained garden soil that is warm. Moreover, because they are a legume and fix nitrogen from the air in the soil, they always improve that soil. For the same reason they need little in the way of artificial fertilizer. Too much, apparently, induces heavy leaf growth and too few pods. On the other hand, heavy composting seems to benefit them no end.

For bush beans, I dig a 2-inch layer of shredded leaves along with a sprinkling of chicken manure and some compost into the top few inches of soil. The manure is to speed up the leaf decay.

About a week later, and when frost no longer threatens, I scatter the seed over a wide bed and lightly press it level with the soil. Next comes a 1-inch covering of dark, mature compost. The almost-black compost readily absorbs heat from the sun to provide an ideal, warm, moist situation for the beans to germinate in.

Depending on the weather, the beans will sprout in 4 to 7 days. Once up and well established, the bean plants should be thinned to one every 10 inches in all directions. Don't thin too quickly, for sometimes the birds do a little thinning of their own when the plants poke through the ground. Once they are about 6 inches tall, I mulch the bed with about an inch of shredded leaves or straw.

Pole Beans

Grow pole beans in single rows up a fence or trellis, spacing the beans 6 inches apart, or in hills up a tripod of wooden stakes. Treat the soil for pole beans the same as for the bush variety. Dig in organic matter, plant the beans, and cover with an inch of compost. Pole beans germinate in 8 to 14 days.

To make the tripods, lash three 8-foot poles together at the top and anchor them 6 inches or more in the ground. Place the poles roughly 30 inches apart at the base. Sow seeds in a circle around each pole. Mulch heavily once the beans are up and climbing. It will help the beans climb tall if the poles are rough, rather than smooth. In other words, if there is bark on the poles, so much the better.

Periodic Feeding

I find that beans respond to periodic foliar feeding with liquid seaweed solution. Around flowering time and when the young beans are forming, I feed the plants with compost water. Simply half fill a bucket with compost, and fill it with water. Stir thoroughly, and let the sediment settle. Draw off the water; it should be the color of weak tea. You can use the compost several times before the tealike strength begins to fade—at which stage throw the sediment back onto the compost heap.

I like to harvest bush beans when they are about as thick as a pencil. They can be left to grow a little larger, but always pick them while they are still crisp enough to snap in your fingers. In harvesting, err if you must on the side of immaturity.

Never cultivate or harvest beans when they are wet as this encourages blight. Watch out for bean beetles, which look like large ladybugs. Hand pick and crush yellow egg clusters laid on the underside of the leaves, or spray with rotenone.

Unearthed: Gardening Secrets for Better Beets

It took me a good many seasons to really appreciate the beet for what it is—a three-in-one vegetable, a genuine must for even the smallest of plots. Limit me to a window box, and I would still sneak in a beet or two somewhere.

Served hot, the beet is a rich red taste treat adding a touch of sweetness to the meal that is matched only by sweet potato, corn, and English peas at their best. Served cold, it adds a new dimension to a tossed salad, and it makes a delectable pickle when marinated for a few hours in vinegar. If that is not enough, its leaves can be served as a green—the perfect substitute for Swiss chard or spinach. Can anyone ask more of a vegetable?

It is relatively simple to grow, too. Frost-tolerant, it is one of the first vegetables to be sown in spring (mine go in along with carrots and cabbage) and one of the last to come out in fall. It thrives best in good rich loam but will grow moderately well in most soils.

Soil Preparation

I mix shredded leaves, compost or old manure, and a little lime into the top few inches of soil and top this off with an inch-thick layer of finely sifted soil to provide a smooth seed bed. I scatter the seed a few inches apart over a broad row and press them into the soil by walking over them on a plank. Then I cover the bed with a ¼- to ½-inch layer of sifted compost. A handful of dried seaweed powder sprinkled over the bed adds additional trace elements. Or you can apply liquid seaweed two or three times during the season.

Each beet seed is actually a fruit containing several minuscule seeds. So it is not uncommon for one fruit to germinate into as many as six beet seedlings. Thinning is a necessity. When the plants are 4 to 6 inches tall, thin to an inch or so apart, and use the thinnings as beet greens. At this stage the tender young leaves make a particularly delicious dish.

Thin again when the roots are about the size of a radish (boil the beets, steam the tops, and combine the two for a gourmet vegetable dish). Continue the thinning process until the plants are about 4 to 6 inches apart. In other words, harvesting from the beet bed is a continual process.

For a regular succession, sow every two weeks from early spring to early summer in the north. A late-summer sowing can produce a good crop of medium-size beets for a fall harvest.

Cold-Weather Vegetable

Beets grow best in cool weather and should never go short of water. Mulch heavily after the second thinning to keep soil cool and moist.

At this stage a little wood ash sprinkled lightly around the plants and watered in supplies additional potash.

Most beet varieties mature about 60 days after germination. There is also a large slow-growing beet, often called a winter keeper, which is worthy of attention. Planted in the late spring, it matures by fall into rough-shaped bulbs 4 to 6 inches across. It is often grown for winter storage because one of its parents is the sugar beet.

You might like to try Burpees Golden, an orange-fleshed, sweet beet that still is unusual enough to be a talking point at the dinner table.

The only pest that bothers the beets in my area is a leaf miner that tunnels its way between the outer membranes of the leaf. It mines the leaf, in other words. Check regularly and squeeze the affected part of the leaf between thumb and forefinger to crush the burrowing grub.

A fail-safe method is to construct an 18-inch-high beet cage (a light box-shaped frame that is covered top and sides with fly screening). Place this over the beets, and the little fly that causes the problem will be unable to get at the beets to lay her eggs.

Pampered Broccoli Will Reward You Well

All last season, from late June through the first deep freeze, we enjoyed fresh-from-the-garden broccoli in our home.

Despite what some garden books suggest is feasible, we regularly cut side heads even during the dog days of late July and August. Then with the cooler days of September these secondary heads became still more abundant and continued that way into November.

Most gardening advice suggests growing a spring crop of broccoli for a June harvest and a second crop (sown in late June here in the north) for a fall crop. That's because this first cousin to the cabbage and the cauliflower develops best in cool weather.

So what kept my broccoli producing small heads clear through the summer? More than anything, I suspect, it was the heavy mulch applied to the plants as soon as they were set out in mid-April. All members of the cabbage family loathe hot roots, but the mulch kept the soil moderate even when day temperatures were consistently in the 80s.

I mulch with shredded leaves because they are free and plentiful. But, if you are prepared to pay for it, alfalfa hay would be even better. Alfalfa is rich in nitrogen, and as it breaks down it feeds this nutrient to the nitrogen-loving broccoli.

For the early crop, buy started plants or sow seed indoors 6 weeks before they go outdoors—around April 15 in my garden. Grow them on a sunny windowsill or 6 to 8 inches below plant lights turned on for 12 to 14 hours.

The seedlings prefer temperatures ranging between 60° and 70° F. When the seedlings are 2½ inches high, thin them to 2 inches apart or transplant into individual containers.

Before setting them in the garden harden the plants for about a week to 10 days. This involves placing them outdoors in moderate sun but protected from wind. Bring them indoors at night.

Another option—one I always follow—is to set the plants straight into the garden and cover them with a plastic milk jug with the cap removed and the bottom cut out, described earlier.

The jugs, made of translucent plastic, temper the sun's rays fractionally while protecting the young plants from windburn. At the same time the open top allows for ventilation. Under these conditions the plants harden off naturally and have no problems adjusting once the jugs are removed.

I plant the seedlings in compost-enriched soil with a sprinkling of wood ash mixed in around each plant. Then they are set out (18 inches apart each way) so that 1 inch of stem protrudes above the soil.

A piece of cardboard wrapped around the stem eliminates the cutworm threat. Then the mulch is spread over the whole bed level with or just above the bottom leaves.

As the plants grow, more mulch is added until at least 4 inches blanket the ground. As this slowly decomposes, I add more mulch materials to maintain the thickness. Remember, the idea is to keep the summer heat out.

Like the rest of the cabbage family, broccoli does not need full sun. Five to six hours a day is sufficient. An ideal position would be where the plants receive early-morning and late-afternoon sun with a nearby tree shading them during the hottest part of the day. In my case last year, the broccoli was shaded from about two o'clock on—another reason, perhaps, that the summer production was better than expected.

When harvesting the main central head, cut only a short stem with it. This leaves a relatively long stem from which the secondary side heads will grow.

After the initial harvest I side-dress the plants with a nitrogen-rich fertilizer. It also helps to apply a manure or compost "tea" to the plants every 2 or 3 weeks throughout the growing season.

One of the drawbacks with broccoli is the little green worms that sometimes lodge themselves deep in the flowery heads. Apply Thuricide during the season. This is a naturally occurring fungus that destroys leaf-eating worms—one of nature's insecticides, you might say.

Cabbage Patch of Which Mrs. Wiggs Could Be Proud

Last year I grew some Savoy King cabbage—the dark green kind with the crinkly leaves—for the first time. In my family's opinion they were the best-tasting *Brassica oleracea capitata* I've grown.

One of the first rules of vegetable gardening is to grow what your family will eat. So the Savoy will feature prominently in my cabbage patch this year. But any cabbage that comes in fresh from the garden—be it Savoy, Copenhagen Market, East Jersey Wakefield, or whatever—has to taste far better than the weeks-old store-bought variety.

There's another good reason why the cabbage and its relatives—broccoli, brussels sprouts, cauliflower, collards, kale, kohlrabi, mustard, and turnips—deserve some corner of your garden: They are among the most nutritious vegetables around.

In a recent study of the forty-two most common fruits and vegetables, the Extension Service of the University of New Hampshire placed all nine members of the cabbage family in the top ten; a proud achievement for the brothers *Brassica*. The sweet pepper was the other top-ten species.

Cabbage started out as a loose-leafed vegetable such as kale is today. It grew wild on England's white cliffs of Dover and in some areas of France and Denmark.

If there is one factor that virtually guarantees a good cabbage crop, it is rich soil. My success last year was due in large part to the barrow load of rabbit manure my neighbor gave me. From the moment I wheeled it into my yard, I knew the cabbages couldn't miss.

I dug in shredded leaves (about a 1-inch layer) and a liberal sprinkling of the manure about a week before setting out the young plants. Then at the bottom of each hole dug to receive the plants, I threw a trowelful of manure and some wood ash, covered this with an inch of soil, and set out the plants.

In the past I've done well by filling the planting holes with compost boosted with a sprinkling of fertilizer. If your fall-harvested cabbages (in the north) can follow a spring crop of peas, so much the better. The peas fix atmospheric nitrogen in the soil, which the cabbages subsequently thrive on.

I plant my cabbages 18 inches apart in three rows 18 inches apart. Lettuce is set out between the cabbages. It grows quickly and is harvested before the large cabbage grows up and needs the space.

Cabbages thrive in cool weather. In the south they are grown in winter for a spring harvest; in the north they grow in spring for an early-summer harvest; and in the late summer and early fall for a mid- to late-fall harvest.

In the north, plant spring cabbage seed indoors 6 to 8 weeks before setting plants out. Harden gradually in a cold frame, and set out once the soil can be worked. I generally wait until the peas have poked through the soil and have begun showing their first leaves around the end of March. I plant seed outdoors for my fall crop around the middle of June and set out the plants toward the end of July or early August.

Plant the seedlings so that about ½ inch of stem shows above the soil. Mulch to keep the soil moist, cool, and free of weeds.

Rough mulching material placed around the base of the plant will also discourage the root maggot. Otherwise, place a square of tar paper on the surface of the soil around each plant. Only once in eight years have I had any root-maggot problems, and that year I did not mulch the cabbage bed. A small twig pushed into the soil on each side of the stem will foil the cutworm.

Begin harvesting the cabbage before all the heads become hard. This way you won't need to harvest all of the crop at once. One way to delay the need to harvest once the heads are mature is to prune the roots of the plant. Place a sharp spade near the stem on one side of the plant, and press down firmly. This will sever some of the roots and cut back the growth rate.

Cabbages That Just Won't Quit

I'd like to introduce you to the cabbages that just wouldn't quit. They grew in our garden last year and fed us all summer long clear through to the first deep freeze.

They were a remarkably productive bunch of *Brassicas*, each one giving us one large head followed by several smaller ones, about the size of softballs.

Now I'd known of this multihead approach for some time, but on the few occasions I experimented with it, I was never over-impressed with the results. Last year's results far exceeded my expectations, so that I intend going the same way again. The secret of this success, I suspect, lay in the rich soil and the thick mulch blanket that was applied to the entire bed.

After harvesting the initial heads, I sprinkled fertilizer around the base of each plant, replaced the mulch, and watered well. Within a week or so the cabbage stalk was surrounded by clusters of small green leaves. I then removed all but two of these (one on each side) and let them develop into hard, softball-size heads.

A Third Crop

Now all I have read on this practice suggests that a second crop is all you can expect from one cabbage plant. But I left them to head up again and harvested two more solid heads from each plant, the latter forming just before the really cold weather of fall set in.

We found the smaller heads were just as tasty as the original large head, though it took two of them for one dinner.

Cabbage enjoys an almost neutral soil, so add lime if yours is on the acid side. The continued addition of compost has brought my originally acid soil to near the neutral line on the pH scale—

a condition in which the acid-loving fungus that causes clubroot in cabbage cannot thrive.

Harvesting Carrots All Year

We had just sat down to dinner—a pot roast with steaming potatoes, green beans, and orange-red carrots glistening in melted butter—when my wife noted that she had just used up the last of our home-grown carrots.

"Enjoy them," she said. "There'll be no more from the garden until this year's crop comes along."

We duly noted that it was May 10, and though none of us was exactly enthusiastic about returning to the store-bought variety, we did note with a sense of gratitude that our backyard plot had supplied us with snapping-crisp carrots for all of nine months.

A gardener's common error (it used to be mine, too) is to grow give-away quantities of summer squash, tomatoes, and other prolific crops but far too few carrots.

Many Uses

Yet consider for a moment how useful carrots are—diced or shredded in a salad, blended with orange juice for a refreshing drink, or steamed and served with melted butter on the dinner plate. And who ever heard of a vegetable soup or stew (at least one worthy of the name) that did not include carrots?

Consider, too, that carrots mature quickly (60 to 70 days after sprouting) and can be sown in northern gardens from early spring into August and over even longer periods in warmer parts of the country.

For a succession of harvests sow every few weeks, the garden books advise. I prefer to sow large quantities in April, June, and then August, when I sow the largest crop of all.

Bed Preparation

I don't do much digging in the garden as a rule, but I do thoroughly prepare the carrot bed. It pays quite handsome dividends. This season, for instance, the selected bed for the first planting (10 feet by 2 feet) was first loosened to a depth of 12 inches. Then three bushel baskets of shredded leaves and another of mature compost were mixed in with the soil.

The leaves and compost quickly disintegrated, adding a light fluffy texture to the soil, which probing carrots thrive on.

The leaf-filled bed was a little too rough for seeds as fine as carrot seeds, so I finally added an inch of topsoil to the surface and tamped this down firmly with the aid of a plank (by walking on it) to make an acceptable seed bed.

After scattering the seeds I covered them with a mixture of soil and peat moss (about half and half) to a depth of about ½ inch.

Careful Watering

Water the seedbed well (every day if the soil is sandy and the weather dry) until the young plants are about 1½ inches tall, by which time the roots will have penetrated to deeper levels where moisture is more stable. In dry spells, soak the bed at least once a week. Lay the hose on the ground, and let the water flow out until the bed is flooded.

Be prepared to thin carrots vigorously; otherwise they will be slow in maturing, and few will attain a decent size. Initial thinning can be done by drawing a garden rake across the bed when the young plants are about 1 inch tall. It appears devastating, but it isn't.

From then on keep pulling the young carrots as soon as they are large enough to eat (½ inch across) until the remaining plants are about 3 inches apart. These will grow large, long, and succulent given good soil.

Incidentally, do not add fresh manure to a carrot bed, as it can burn young roots and also causes the skin to grow rough and hard. If you have little or no compost, apply a light sprinkling of a balanced (preferably natural) fertilizer.

Sand-Seed Mix

Carrot seeds are so fine it is difficult to distribute them evenly over the soil. One helpful practice is to thoroughly mix 1 ounce of seed in one or two cups of fine sand or sifted compost before sowing. Another is to buy pelleted seeds. The seeds are coated with white clay so that they are large enough to handle easily (about the size of a radish seed) and readily stand out against the dark soil. The result for me has been relatively even spacing so that I don't need to do any thinning, at least until the carrots are substantial enough to eat.

Our winter crops are sown early in August, mulched with shredded leaves when the cold weather arrives, and finally covered with bags of leaves just before the soil starts to freeze. This practice effectively insulates the soil here in Massachusetts so that the crop can be harvested as needed throughout the winter.

I lift all remaining carrots in March and store them in damp sand in the coolest part of the cellar.

A More Efficient Cauliflower Gains Ground

Around the time of year when snow blankets the garden and wind rattles the gaunt apple branches, it seems difficult to believe spring will ever come. But the newly arrived seed catalogs insist it will, and so I plan what crops will go where in my garden and when.

Frequently, I look around for something new to try, and this year I am opting for green cauliflowers. That's right, green cauliflowers. From all accounts they are delicious.

I became interested in them after I met their developer, Michigan State University plant breeder Shigemi Honma. He's the man who developed the self-blanching cauliflower, among others.

Dr. Honma was looking for a way to eliminate the labor involved in tying up the heads of white cauliflower so that the curds would not turn yellow. So he thought of making the heads green. After all, he reasoned, most folks who like cauliflower like the taste of green broccoli. So he simply crossed the two; or rather, through eight generations he kept crossing back and forth until the Michigan Agricultural Experiment Station had a product it could be proud of.

Chartreuse to Start

Green Ball, as the variety is known, is an attractive chartreuse that turns pale green when cooked. It is finely textured and a top-quality eating product. Another plus: it is less odoriferous than its white counterpart.

But commercial growers didn't take avidly to the green cauliflower (they tend to be followers rather than leaders when something this different comes along) and saw no reason for it at all when Dr. Honma followed up with a self-blanching conventional cauliflower.

Subsequently, the green cauliflower has had some success as a novelty item in Canada and the United States, and home gardeners who try it generally give it good marks.

Other Varieties

More common than the green cauliflower is the purple variety. But the head of the purple type is more coarse, closely resembling broccoli. When cooked the purple head turns green.

In contrast to the green variety, Dr. Honma's self-blanching cauliflower became an immediate success. It eliminated the labor of tying up the heads while producing a conventional white head that needed no testing on the consumer market.

This variety produces a jacket of inner leaves that curls around the cauliflower head (much as a man might place his hands on his head). This excludes the light and results in a snow white head.

Saves Labor

Commercial growers enjoy this variety because the labor of tying up cauliflower heads can sometimes run to 70% of production costs. Even home gardeners benefit because a head left untied or poorly tied for even a few days results in rapid yellowing of the curds. This doesn't mean that they are any less tasty; they just don't look as good.

One word of warning about the self-blanching cauliflower: In hot weather it doesn't do what it is supposed to do. The protecting leaves curl over very effectively only when heads form in the cooler days of early fall in the north. In parts of southern Florida they will not do so even in winter.

Garden Too Small for Corn? Don't You Believe It

If your garden is small, don't plant corn. That's standard (if irritating) gardening advice. But who really wants to heed it?

Let's face it—few treats come out of a garden to match freshly picked corn, so that even a dozen or so homegrown ears are worth the effort. Moreover, there are proven ways to include corn in otherwise fully occupied areas.

Maize, as the rest of the world terms corn, is a truly American plant—South American to be exact. It was being cultivated by the Indians two thousand years ago, and over the centuries it spread northward across the Isthmus of Panama into North America, whose cornfields now feed much of the world.

Now, with hybridized short-season varieties available, the northern limit of this heat-loving plant has moved well beyond the Canadian border.

Better in Rich Soil

Corn will grow satisfactorily in average garden soil, but it will thrive in organically rich soil. So the more compost and manure you can pile on the corn plot, the better.

Given plenty of space you might try growing your corn in double rows 12 inches apart with about 3 feet between each double row.

Another method that appeals to me was devised by the late Sam Ogden of Landgrove, Vermont. First, mark off the plot in 30-inch squares. In the center of each square take out a shovelful of earth and fill the hole with compost, tamping it down with the back of a hoe. Then cover the compost with half of the dug-out soil.

Next, walk through the corn plot dropping four to six seeds in each planting spot or hill. The remaining loose soil is then spread over the seeds so that they are roughly 1 inch deep.

After germination each hill is thinned to three plants.

Mulch corn lightly once the soil has warmed up; when the plants are knee high, add more mulch—straw, leaves, or well-rotted manure—to a depth of 6 inches.

The old belief that corn likes sun on its roots has long been disproved. Folks who have tested it out have found the mulched section of their corn patch has consistently outyielded the unmulched section.

Corn is a broad-leaved plant that needs plenty of water if it is to grow rapidly—hence, the great value of a thick mulch. It prevents the soil from drying out and readily absorbs rainwater, which it steadily releases to the plant. A thick mulch also braces the tall, slender stalks against the onslaught of high winds.

The problem with corn is that it consumes a lot of space relative to the yield. So where does this leave the gardener with a small plot? Well, a regular corn patch can be justified by intercropping with some quick-growing crop such as beets or lettuce.

These are harvested before the corn grows large enough to need all the space.

Another approach is to combine corn with climbing runner beans. To do this the corn rows or hills will have to be somewhat more widely spaced to allow enough sun to get in for the beans' liking.

Simply plant the beans around the hills or alongside the rows. The climbing vines get their support from the cornstalks without hindering the corn's development. They yield well enough, and there is considerable evidence to suggest that the nitrogen fixed in the soil by the beans stimulates corn growth.

Isolated Clumps

Yet another small-garden option, which has worked well for me, is the isolated-clump method. After the rest of the garden has been planned, look around for patches of unused space, and treat them as Mr. Ogden does. This way, picturesque clumps of corn sprout in the garden near the summer squash, alongside the rhubarb, between the blueberry bushes, wherever there's a square foot or so of unused space.

High Time to Start Growing the Lowly Cucumber

I've seen folks search the supermarket for the largest cucumber they could find. Incredibly, I've also known of some gardeners who put size ahead of taste in the cukes they grow at home.

To put it most charitably, both practices are unwise. But while the shopper gets volume, if very little value, for his money, the gardener forfeits both quality and quantity by this approach.

In the vegetable garden, biggest isn't always best—and with cucumbers it never is. In fact, the smaller they are picked, within reason, the better they taste and the more cucumbers, by weight, the vine will produce.

The purpose of each cucumber vine is to reproduce itself; and once it has borne a few large fruits, each filled with mature (and tough to eat) seeds, it has done its job and can take early retirement. In contrast, the vine that has been unable to produce mature seeds goes on trying, which is just what every good gardener wants it to do.

Origin in India

The cucumber originally grew wild along the banks of India's Ganges River, from which it was taken to the gardens of China. The Chinese, in turn, presented it to Europe, from which it quickly hopped the Atlantic.

Columbus, it is said, brought the cuke to Cuba, where the Indians were quick to accept the new plant. By the time the Pilgrims crossed the Atlantic, cucumbers were a regular crop in New England.

The original home of the cucumber indicates the conditions the vine likes best—warm to hot weather with a readily available supply of moisture. The silt-laden banks of the Ganges are also very fertile, and cukes everywhere grow best in compost- and fertilizer-enriched soil.

In heavy clay soils that do not drain well, it is recommended that cucumbers be grown in mounds so that standing water does not collect around the stems. In contrast, I grew some of my best cukes last year in a trench, which guaranteed that all water would collect and sink in right around the plants. The soil in my garden, however, is very light and drains rapidly.

The best cucumbers I ever saw were growing in a garden of a friend in Clinton, Connecticut. Emil Dahlquist grows his vines in mounded rows with a series of 2-pound cans, perforated below soil level, sunk halfway into the soil to aid in irrigation.

Here's How

The method works this way: First, compost and manure are worked liberally into the soil, which is then mounded roughly 6 inches high and 12 to 15 inches broad at the base. Each mounded row is 4 feet apart. The seeds are sown an inch deep along the top of the mound between the cans, which are spaced every 18 inches along the row.

The perforated part of the can is sunk into the soil so that all water poured into the cans is forced into the soil, rather than allowed to run off it. Later, when the plants are up and growing, Mr. Dahlquist puts a little manure and/or compost into the cans, in effect producing a liquid fertilizer every time he waters.

A variation on the same theme is to sink a 5-pound can into the soil and sow the seeds in a circle around it. These "hills," as gardening books term them, can be mounded or level with the surrounding soil.

Cucumbers are deep-rooted plants that respond well to generous organic matter—particularly if the soil is light and sandy. For an extra-special crop, dig a hole or trench 2 feet deep, half fill it with compost, old manure, rotting hay, or sawdust (or a mixture), and top with soil that includes some finely sifted compost. Otherwise, incorporate a little fertilizer in this topsoil a week or two before planting.

Cukes are frost-tender, so standard gardening advice is that seeds be sown only after all danger of frost has passed. But there are ways of getting a jump on the seasons. Vermont gardener and author Dick Raymond takes the following tack to beat late frosts in his state: First, he sprouts the seeds indoors in several layers of damp paper toweling. Then he carefully sows the sprouted seed outdoors under hotcaps (plastic milk jugs with the bottoms removed will do) and leaves the caps in place until warm weather has arrived to stay.

It would help, too, to lay a sheet of clear plastic over the bed where the cukes will grow several weeks ahead of time. This will help warm up the soil to the cukes' liking.

If left to sprawl, cucumber vines take up a lot of garden space. So grow them up a fence or trellis. Or you might try what I plan to do this season: grow them inside circular cages as is sometimes done in tomato culture.

Hothouses for Cucumbers from Old Auto Tires

A neighbor of mine threw out a couple of old tires the other day, and I could kick myself for not having grabbed them before the rubbish pickup came along.

You see, I have just discovered use in the food garden for the otherwise useless tire—as a hothouse for cucumber vines. New Hampshire farmers Leandre and Gretchen Poisson say they have upped the productivity of their vines considerably since they began bedding down their cukes inside tires.

This is how the Poissons go about it. They place the tires alongside each other on a prepared bed and plant a few cucumber seeds in each enclosed circle, covering the tires afterward with clear plastic to create a greenhouse effect.

The soil quickly warms up in this situation, and the heat absorbed by the tires during the day is radiated to keep the tender plants warm at night. This way the Poissons get a jump of several weeks on the season in their part of New Hampshire.

Tires Stay Put

By the time the vines are pushing up against the plastic, the weather is generally warm enough for the plastic to be removed. The tires stay in place, however, so that they will continue to raise the temperature around the vines at night and thus speed up the growth. One other advantage: the tires dam water around the vines when they are irrigated so that it is forced to sink in right around the roots. To increase the heat retention of the tires, Mr. Poisson suggests filling them with stones before setting them in place.

The Poissons have the space to let their cucumbers trail. In more compact gardens it might be good to train the vines up a trellis or perhaps a tomato cage, which could be placed either inside or outside the tire.

For Tomatoes, Too

What is good for cukes should be good for other heat-loving plants, too. Tomatoes are one obvious example. Tender seedlings could be set out under plastic weeks ahead of the normal date. A second tire could be stacked on top of the first as the tomato grows and the resulting container filled with soil or compost as the plant grows. This would allow a strong root system to form all the way up the buried stem. The Poissons, in fact, plan to extend tire cultivation to their tomato crop regularly.

Other heat-loving crops include the pepper, eggplant, and all members of the cucurbit family, including melons and squash.

Tires also make it possible to grow food crops on stony, tree-root-infested, and steeply sloping ground as well. On rocky or rooty soil, stack tires three layers high and fill with compost enriched soil to start a container garden. One gardener I know claims the stacked-tire method produces the best early potato crops, possibly because of warmer growing conditions in the early spring.

On steep slopes drive a short stake into the ground, and hang the tire around this. Now fill the tire to the level of the lower side of the tire to form a flat planting bed.

You should have no trouble getting old tires. Tire merchants usually have a hard time getting rid of them.

Every Gardener Needs Herbs

I once had the pleasure of watching Swiss master chef Arthur Moergeli prepare one of his *nouvelle cuisine* dishes during a tour of the United States.

Leeks, carrots, chicken breasts, and shrimp were the featured ingredients. But just as important were the small quantities of herbs that added a piquancy and flavor that simply wouldn't have existed without them.

As he ground up the herbs in a pestle and mortar, the chef made this comment: "A cook is a cook but never a chef until he knows the wise use of herbs."

This got me to thinking. Perhaps a similar judgment could be made of the food gardener who didn't bother with an herb garden. For years I grew vegetables but relied on the supermarket for needed herbs until I sought some advice from John Scarchuk, a lecturer in plant science at the University of Connecticut.

In colonial times, according to Mr. Scarchuk, a kitchen garden wasn't considered a kitchen garden "unless it had a good selection of culinary or savory herbs."

In the absence of refrigeration, winter menus particularly had to rely on the same old fare day after day. One way of breaking the monotony was by changing the herbs. It was also said that herbs could mask a stale or slightly "off" taste that frequently turned up in those days of no refrigeration.

Symbiotic Benefits

Recently, however, cooks and epicures have begun rediscovering the subtle flavors of herbs that for so long have been lacking in modern cooking. There is, said Mr. Scarchuk, a "turning again to old recipes that call for the use of herbs."

For the gardener there is another plus to growing herbs: they add a fragrance otherwise missing from the largely scentless vegetable plot and through a symbiotic relationship frequently stimulate vegetable growth. Basil, for instance, is said to enhance the growth of neighboring tomato plants.

Herbs can be beautiful, too. The red dark-opal strain of basil can serve purely as an ornamental foliage plant, as can chives, thyme, sage, and summer and winter savory in an ornamental garden.

Mr. Scarchuk suggested starting with the six herbs named by the French *les fines herbes*—sweet basil, chervil, sweet marjoram, thyme, rosemary, and tarragon. Other important ones are chives, parsley, summer savory, dill, and the mints—peppermint, spearmint, winter savory, sage, and burnet. In the end, however, your choice of herbs will depend on your family's preferences.

In general, a few rows of each annual and about half a dozen perennials will provide enough herbs for an average family. But rather than grow them all together you might consider dotting them about your vegetable and flower garden. Spread the fragrance around, in other words.

Seed for annuals is available from garden supply centers; perennials are propagated by cuttings, and you should get your initial plant from a nursery.

Soil Requirements

Most herbs grow successfully under a wide range of soil conditions; but sage, rosemary, and thyme require a well-drained, moderately moist situation, while parsley, chervil, and mints do best in heavier soils that retain considerable moisture. All herbs except mint require a sunny exposure.

Average fertility gives good results, but heavy fertilizing will produce heavy growth at the expense of flavor.

Herbs are richest in the volatile oils that impart flavor and fragrance just before flowering. Harvest at this stage unless, as with dill, it is the fruit you are seeking. The old method of drying (and still a good one) is to tie the herbs in bunches and hang them in an attic. Or spread them on the rack of an oven under a very low heat. Never dry herbs in the sun, as this robs them of the very volatile oils that give the herbs their flavor. Strip the leaves from the stems when they are crunchy dry, and store in a well-labeled glass or metal container.

If fresh green tips are used, preserve them in vinegar. Dark-opal basil will color white vinegar a beautiful ruby red color. When the potency of the herbs has been absorbed in the vinegar after a week or two, the herbs may be removed.

Leeks—Worth Cost, Effort: the Gourmet's Onion

One Sunday evening recently my wife suggested that creamed leeks would go well with the omelet she was planning for supper. So I went out and dug up half a dozen or so.

At the time I was unaware (but found out at the supermarket the next day) that a gourmet price tag is attached to this relative of the onion family. In fact, I am told they are never cheap even when they are at their most plentiful in the fall.

So, delighted at how cheaply we had eaten so expensive a dish, I returned to the garden the next day to evaluate what was left of the leek bed. It came to more than $25—in about 11 square feet of bed. Now that's a lot of money in a little space, I feel. Certainly, we would not eat leeks with such abandon if we had to go out and buy them.

You can substitute leeks in any dish calling for onions, and you will find, by the way, that you won't cry when peeling or dicing them. Another leek advantage: it can stay outdoors (properly mulched) all winter long. All told, then, it's a most suitable vegetable for the home garden.

For my part, I like to start seeds indoors for a late-summer crop. Seeds sown outdoors in May provide the fall and winter leeks.

Now if there is one ingredient for success with leeks it is the generous application of compost. They thrive on it as few other plants do. So I dig a narrow trench about 4 inches deep and incorporate compost in the bottom. The young plants are set out 4 inches apart in this trench. As they grow, I fill in with a rich mixture of compost and soil (or all compost if there is enough on hand) around the stems. This forces the plants to grow tall and the stems to blanch. After the trench is filled, I mound shredded leaves around the stems to continue the blanching process.

Another advantage of this mounding is that it locks heat into the soil around the plants, enabling them to continue growing until the really cold weather of late December arrives. This way, I was able to harvest one leek (I must confess no other came close) that had a stem measuring 14 inches long by 1½ inches in diameter.

In cold areas such as New England, storing vegetables for the winter months is always something of a problem. So the more vegetables that can be left right out in the garden, the better. Along with parsnips and carrots, add leeks to the list of vegetables hardy enough to endure such treatment.

Fill in between the leeks with shredded leaves or straw. Then when really cold weather arrives throw bags loosely filled with leaves on top. This is a very effective insulation, and here in the Boston area I was able to dig leeks up all winter long without any effort.

One smaller bed of leeks, however, was insufficiently mulched so that the top 2 to 3 inches of soil had become frozen. It took a pickax to harvest them. Even so, they appeared largely unaffected by the freeze and were perfectly edible. On the other hand, complete exposure to freezing weather will destroy leeks.

❧

Lettuce Grows Best in Soft Nitrogen-Rich Soil

The best head of lettuce I ever grew—cabbage-size, and that's no exaggeration—was in soil on which chickens had run around for the best part of a decade.

Over the years a good deal of straw litter had combined with the manure to break down into a fabulously rich, humus-filled soil in which any lettuce seed of reasonable lineage could not possibly fail.

Ever since then, I've tried to repeat the conditions in that chicken run. And if I've come marginally close, the lettuce has been good. In short, head lettuce does best in soft soil that is rich in nitrogen. It likes what cabbage likes.

Thousands of years ago ancient Chinese civilizations prized the lettuce. Before 500 B.C. Persian kings served it on the royal table. Aristotle took time out from philosophizing to praise the practical and delectable lettuce. But it was left to more recent generations to induce certain lettuce strains to form a crisp, compact head.

Three Kinds Planted

In my garden I grow three lettuce strains—Ithaca, a crisp tight-heading variety generally carried by supermarkets, Buttercrunch, a more loose-heading Bibb-type, and an heirloom loose-leaf variety called Black Seeded Simpson, which, in my view, has the most tender, best-tasting leaves of the lot. They all grow well together.

The Ithaca lettuce seedlings are set out 15 inches apart with a Buttercrunch or Black Seeded Simpson in between. The Buttercrunch, which form small heads quickly, are harvested first, leaving space for the larger Ithaca to grow into. Is there a better intercropping combination?

As much compost and manure as I can spare are forked lightly into the rows where the lettuce will be set out a week later. Then at planting time I place a trowelful of manure at the bottom of each hole, topped by about an inch of soil. This assures each plant of a goodly supply of nitrogen—so important to vigorous growth. Rabbit and chicken manures are best for lettuce. Cow manure, with a sprinkling of blood meal, works well, too. Another good nitrogen source is cottonseed meal.

Cool-Weather Crop

Lettuce is a cool-weather crop. So in the south it is grown from late fall through early spring. In the north it grows in spring and fall—and all summer long in those rare areas where moisture-laden sea breezes moderate the temperature.

Here in Massachusetts, I start my seed indoors about 4 weeks before the young seedlings are set out. In other words, I sow in early March for an April planting. When the plants are set out, more seed is sown outdoors for a successive crop. Seed for the fall crop is sown outdoors in the first part of August. Transplanting helps in forming good heads. This is because the transplanting shock encourages the development of a strong root system. I sow the seed in a flat; then I transplant the young plants into other flats before finally setting them out. Seedlings sown directly outdoors are transplanted only once, from seedbed to growing bed.

Harden Seedlings

A week before setting the young plants outdoors, harden them off a little by lowering night temperatures and by watering less frequently. Allow the surface of the soil to dry out before giving them more water, but no good is accomplished by allowing plants to wilt from thirst. Finally, water the transplants thoroughly an hour or so before setting them out. When transplanting, remove the outer leaves of the young plant.

There are several ways to outwit the cutworm. A piece of paper wrapped around the stem forms a suitable protective collar. A twig pushed into the ground right next to the stem is effective. I often bury a tuna fish or cat food can with top and bottom removed and plant the seedling in this.

I cover the little lettuce plants when first set out with a gallon-size plastic milk jug from which the cap and bottom have been removed. This protects the plants from wind while they become established. At the same time the somewhat cloudy plastic lets in all the light a young plant needs while filtering out some of the sun's heat.

Lettuce is a rapid grower, hence the need for a nutrient-rich soil and plenty of moisture. See that the beds are well watered, particularly when the heads begin to form. A straw or shredded-leaf mulch is beneficial both for keeping the roots cool and for conserving soil moisture.

You might try growing lettuce all summer long by shading it under a framework covered with two layers of cheesecloth or a combination of latticework and cheesecloth.

Raising a Bushel of Onions in Your Backyard

A nineteenth-century gourmet expressed my sentiments exactly when he said: "Without the onion there would be no gastronomic art. Banish it from the kitchen and all pleasure of eating flies with it. . . . Its absence reduces the rarest dainty to insipidity, and the diner to despair."

Apparently, this love affair with onions extends back into pre-history. Onions, according to inscriptions, fed the toiling builders of the pyramids, and the conquering armies of Alexander the Great ate onions all the way to India. More recently, General Ulysses S. Grant wrote the War Department: "I will not move my armies without onions."

Now home gardeners do not have to feed armies (even if at times it may seem like it), so a relatively small onion patch can contribute significantly to the family larder. One summer I harvested a little more than two bushel baskets from a 4-by-10-foot patch.

Feed and Water Well

If there is one secret to growing onions (including garlic, shallots, leeks, and bunching onions), it is to feed and water them well. They are heavy feeders, and because they have shallow roots, they need moisture near the surface of the soil.

Dig in as much compost or manure (or both) as you can spare—up to about 3 pounds per square foot if your soil is poor. If the manure is fresh, turn it into the soil at least 2 weeks before planting.

For my part I spread an inch or so of mature compost over the whole bed and plant onion sets directly into this compost.

One year I sprinkled some 5-10-10 fertilizer over half the onion bed and found it made no difference to the production, suggesting that the 1-inch compost layer was adequate. Without compost, however, I would probably incorporate 4 to 5 pounds of balanced fertilizer per 100 square feet on the garden about a week before planting.

Seed, Plants, or Sets

You can grow onions from seed, started plants, or sets (small onions about the size of a dime). I have grown my largest onions from seed by starting them indoors in winter. Nursery-bought plants have done well, too, but invariably I've lost some to cold spring winds. Sets are by far the easiest to work with and can be harvested early enough in my area (late July) so that a late quick-growing crop can follow. Last year I followed the onions with snap beans, peas, and a row of brussels sprout seedlings. Carrots and beets are other alternatives.

In early spring I plant the sets in wide beds, leaving about 2 inches between each set. As the plants grow, I thin out the bed, using the thinnings as scallions. The sets are pressed into the soil so that just the top is left protruding. Too-deep planting results in thick stems (perfectly edible but no good for storing) and no bulbs.

Keep Weeds Out

Weeds should be kept out of the patch—a tiresome but rewarding task. On the other hand, I have read of one gardener who avoids weeds with a newspaper mulch. He spreads wet newspaper, a few sheets thick, over the plot and then makes little holes where he plants the onions. It works very well apparently, and the newspaper slowly decomposes as the onions grow.

Onions grow tops in cool weather and form bulbs when it is hot. When half or more of the onion tops have fallen, the remaining upright tops should be pressed over. This stops any further top growth and adds size to the bulbs. When the tops eventually turn brown, pull the onions and let the roots dry out and become brittle.

I leave my onions to dry for about 2 weeks on a wire screen, after which they are stored in a cool place in wire baskets where the air can freely circulate.

An Easier Way to Plant Onions

There is, by the way, a much quicker way to plant onion sets than pressing them carefully into the soil one by one. It might be termed the scatter-and-mulch method, and it's the only way to go if you're planting a lot at one time.

After spreading compost, I sprinkle the sets over the surface as evenly as possible—though there's no need to be too fussy in this regard. Next, using a piece of plank, I gently press them into the compost just as they lie. Then I cover them with an inch or so of shredded leaves or up to 3 inches of loose hay, water well, and forget about them for a while.

Even firming the little bulbs into the soil isn't all that necessary. In the moist but airy conditions under the mulch the elongated sets that are lying on their sides will send out roots, right themselves, and grow as well as any planted with more deliberation.

The mulch, which is the key to this easy planting method, also performs another labor-saving service: it cuts down on weeds. If, as the season progresses, the mulch wears thin in places, add a little more.

For a Long-Running Onion Try Planting Egyptians

Thanks to a friend who gave me a handful of bulblets a couple of years ago, we never go short of onions for soups, stews, salads, or sauces.

The onions in question are the Egyptian variety that increases by division and by producing small onion sets at the top of its leaves. It's unquestionably one of the most efficient of the multiplier onions.

Egyptians meet our onion needs for much of the year. They are the first spring vegetable to be harvested in cold northern climates, and they continue producing right through until the first freeze comes along.

Don't expect large bulbs from this onion. It produces an elongated bulb and, given enough space and rich soil, will grow to about 1 inch in diameter and 3 inches long before dividing to form two plants.

The Scallion Way

During July the bulblets or sets that form at the top of the plant mature. The supporting stem falls over, and the bulblets root to form another cluster of onions alongside the parent plant. Left this way, your Egyptian onion bed soon becomes overcrowded, and no onion grows thicker than a pencil, which is great for scallions but not much more.

To get large scallions, I plant Egyptian onions this way: After enriching the soil with compost or manure, I dig a trench about 4 inches deep, and push the bulblet about an inch into the soil. As it grows I fill in with soil or compost until the trench is filled up. Then I add mulch for another 2 to 3 inches.

When freezing weather threatens, I pile on more mulch, about 8 to 12 inches. In early spring the green shoots poke through this mulch, and harvesting can begin right then. Dig deeply, using a narrow-tined instrument. If you try to pull them up, you will merely snap off the tops.

During the growing season these individual plants increase by division, so that soon you have a clump of onions. When we dig up a clump, we simply push one onion plant back into the soil (about 4 inches deep), and a new clump quickly forms.

Even more than conventional onions Egyptians seem to develop a strong flavor if they lack moisture. So water them well in dry weather, being careful to see that the water soaks in deeply. Nothing could be worse for this onion than soil that is muddy on the surface but dry around the roots.

Folks who have these multiplier onions usually have sets or spare plants to give away—often because they have let them grow out of hand. On the other hand, you can try getting some from nurseries specializing in bulbs.

Parsnips—a Hardy, Tasty Garden Crop

When my favorite garden catalog arrives, I immediately open it to section P. There, immediately after parsley but ahead of peas, peppers, and pumpkins, is the vegetable I want: parsnips. Though I have a grandparent who hailed from parsnip-loving Wales, I confess I discovered the vegetable only recently.

A neighbor who had grown a pretty good crop gave us some along with a recipe for parsnip stew. The stew turned out to be something of a gourmet treat, in our opinion, and even our daughters (notoriously suspicious of anything new) ate it without comment. The parsnips also tasted very good boiled, baked, or fried. In other words, they became a must for our own garden.

So one spring we put in a trial bed of these white, carrot-shaped vegetables. They flourished, and before Christmas I pulled back the leaves that were protecting them and dug just two. They weighed exactly 1 and 1½ pounds, respectively—more than enough for the hearty stew my wife had planned for that evening.

Such generous rewards for the labor involved are nothing short of a delight to any gardener. I am now totally sold on the sweet white roots. Hence the haste with which I turn to the catalog and make the notation "two packets" alongside the entry marked parsnips.

That's right—I hope for double the crop from now on, for its hardiness enables it to grow well into the fall and stay in the ground untroubled by freezing all winter long. The colder it gets, the sweeter the parsnips become, which is why many New England gardeners insist on waiting clear through till spring before digging them.

On the other hand, experienced parsnip growers will tell you that they are pretty sweet even before the first frost and that there is no harm in harvesting some of them early.

Parsnips are native to both North America and Europe, and they were harvested long before the Roman Emperor Tiberius found them as good a reason as any to have his legionnaires stationed in Germany.

Like carrots, to which they are related, parsnips thrive in deeply dug soil. Unlike carrots, they are slow growers, taking around four months to mature. Here in New England I plant mine around the first week in May.

Dig the soil over to a depth of at least 12 inches, remove the stones, and incorporate as much compost or well-rotted cow manure as you can spare. Add a balanced garden fertilizer (1 pound per approximately 30 square feet) if your compost stocks are low.

Sow parsnips in furrows about half an inch deep and cover with finely sifted compost or peat moss. Be prepared to wait a little. The seeds can take as long as 3 weeks to germinate. Thin to around 4 inches apart.

Once established, the parsnips send their roots deep into the soil to gather moisture. Before that time be sure to keep the soil moist at all times.

How to Grow a Bumper Crop of Peas

My wife brought a bowlful of steaming peas with a golden butter patty on top to the table last night. They were honey-sweet to the taste and almost as quickly as the butter melted, the peas disappeared from our plates.

Of all this world's vegetables, the green pea is the most universally popular. That's because of its sweetness. Indeed, fully one-quarter by weight of fresh peas is vegetable sugar. But, as in sweet corn, this sugar quickly turns to starch after picking or if left to grow old on the vine. The need, then, is to eat or freeze green peas within a day of picking.

Pisum sativum, as the botanists call it, is native to Europe, northern Asia, and parts of Africa. In Ethiopia the wild ancestor of the pea can still be found in some highland areas.

When William the Conqueror invaded England in 1066, he noted that peas were a regular crop in monastery gardens. And by the time the Pilgrims sailed to America in 1620, the English had perfected the modern-day pea. Hence the term English pea, used in the United

States to differentiate it from the black-eyed or southern peas grown in hot climates.

Peas are a cool-weather crop and are the first seeds I sow here in Massachusetts. In the north they are a spring crop; in the south, sow them in the fall for an early winter harvest as I used to do when living in Africa.

Peas prefer a sandy loam soil rich in humus. So dig in compost, rotting hay, or leaf mold when preparing the bed. Do this just as soon as the frost is out of the ground and the soil dry enough to dig without turning to mud.

Because they are legumes, peas require little nitrogen but appreciate both phosphate and potash. Good compost is ideal. So is cow manure. Save the wood ash from your winter fires, and sprinkle it on the soil to provide additional potash. If you have none of these materials, a light application of 5-10-10 fertilizer applied a week before planting will help.

Coat the seed with a legume inoculant just before sowing. This makes certain that the colonies of bacteria that help gather in free nitrogen from the air will establish themselves in the plant's roots. If you have grown legumes in the same spot before, however, the beneficial bacteria will still be there in the soil.

Most garden books suggest sowing peas 1 inch deep and 3 inches apart in single rows. I prefer broad-row sowing. Last year, for instance, I scattered the seed roughly 6 inches apart in all directions in beds between 3 and 5 feet wide.

After scattering the seed, I pressed them into the loose soil by placing a plank on the bed and walking on it. Then I covered the seeds with about an inch of shredded leaves. Compost would do just as well. Being sturdy plants, the young peas have no trouble pushing up through the mulch.

Single-row plants need wire netting, small branches, or similar support on which the vines can climb. In broad-row plantings the vines largely support themselves, although I find it helps to provide some support along the outside edges of the bed.

In spring, there is usually a good deal of moisture in the soil; but should spring rains fail, give your peas regular watering. Moisture is particularly important when pods are beginning to form.

I mention that peas need cool weather in which to grow. Yet one variety, Wando, tolerates heat better than others.

How to Grow Peas with a Minimum of Fuss

I learned a little trick with garden peas the other day that promises not only a bountiful harvest but easy pickings as well. It involves newspapers and the productive little bush pea, Sparkle.

Dick Willard, who showed me how it works, isn't a household word among home gardeners. But in the seed trade he's well known for his association with the oldest continuously operating seed company in these United States—Comstock Ferry Company of Wethersfield, Connecticut.

Now it is not uncommon in the garden industry for some folks to be too busy telling others how to grow things to do any gardening themselves—and that includes a few garden writers, too. But that doesn't apply to seedsman Willard. He gardens even when he doesn't have the time!

The Full Freezer

I knew instantly that Dick Willard was an accomplished grower of food crops the moment I sneaked a look into his freezer. It was pretty well filled with garden produce—green peas particularly. He had enough packages of frozen peas to satisfy his immediate family—and I suspect a few in-laws as well—clear through to the next harvest.

"How do you do it?" I asked. "With a little compost, a little fertilizer, and lots of newspaper," he grinned.

After preparing the soil in the spring by adding compost and a light application of a balanced fertilizer, Mr. Willard covers the entire bed with newspapers ten or more pages thick, leaving a ½-inch gap where the rows of peas will be sown. The papers have been presoaked so that they lie flat and don't blow around in the wind. They are placed so that each ½-inch gap, or row, is spaced 12 inches apart.

The peas then are sown by pressing them about an inch into the soil. At this stage Mr. Willard waters them well and, in effect, leaves them to grow while he goes about his seed business.

The paper mulch does several good things for young pea vines. First, it eliminates all weeds except the few that might spring up in the rows; second, it keeps the root area moist and cool—conditions in which peas thrive; and, third, it provides additional reflected light at a period in the year when overcast days can be plentiful.

As they grow, the vines spread out, completely hiding the newspapers.

Efficiency, Plus

Now comes the easy-picking part of the story. By choosing a dwarf variety, such as Sparkle, which matures the bulk of its pods all at once, Mr. Willard can harvest the entire crop in one fell swoop. He does this by pulling up the vines and repairing to the patio, where he sits in comfort and picks one vine at a time.

It's a whole lot faster to pick peas from your lap than to stoop over a row in the garden. "You can do a better job, too," he says, "because you're less likely to miss any peas this way."

Mr. Willard waits until a few pods "are a little past their prime before harvesting. Then I know that the majority are just right."

Now the value of the newspaper mulch doesn't end with the pea harvest. It goes right on doing a fine job for the rest of the season.

In the Willard garden this year, the peas were followed with a late cabbage, cauliflower, and brussels sprout crop, due to mature with the arrival of the first frost. These *Brassicas* reveled in the nitrogen put into the soil by the leguminous peas and rejoiced in the still weed-free environment provided by the newspapers.

All season long the earthworms feast on the newspaper at the soil surface, so that by fall they have reduced it to a thin layer. At this stage it is tilled into the soil along with other garden waste in readiness for the following season.

Try Growing Potatoes on or above the Ground

I've chatted with many gardeners, and most of them agree that the potato is the most exciting crop in the vegetable plot. Harvesting it is somewhat like opening a present on Christmas Day: you expect something good, but you never know for sure until you've removed the wrapping.

In my garden "unwrapping" the potatoes means pulling aside the leaves, straw, or other mulching materials to reveal a cluster of gleaming white- or red-skinned tubers that usually range from the larger bakers down to golfball-size.

Ever since I began growing potatoes above the ground rather than in it, I've harvested a reasonably uniform crop each year. I wouldn't grow them any other way unless I was short on the necessary mulching materials.

Yankee Ingenuity

Early Yankee farmers, often with more leaves available to them than stone-free soil, discovered that some good crops of potatoes could be grown right in mounds of leaves. Then as farming moved to the rich soil of the Midwest, the idea fell into disuse. But it has revived in recent years with the return of backyard gardening.

I have grown the ever-popular spud in leaves, on the ground with a covering of leaves, and once on a patch of lawn with a leaf-straw covering. All harvests were satisfactory. But the best crop came when the seed potatoes were shallowly planted in well-prepared soil and allowed to grow up through a thick mulch.

My present practice is to incorporate shredded leaves in the bed with a little old horse manure or cow manure, if I can get it. A week or so later I make shallow trenches in the bed and plant the seed potatoes 10 inches apart in back-to-back rows 12 inches apart. In wider beds the rows are 1½ to 2 feet apart.

Whole Seed Potatoes

I prefer whole seed potatoes about the size of a hen's egg; otherwise, I cut larger potatoes into pieces, each containing three eyes from which the stems will sprout.

The potatoes are pressed level with the soil and covered with an inch or so of mature compost. When the potatoes are between 6 and 8 inches tall, I mulch heavily with shredded leaves, pine needles, and straw, virtually covering the young plants. During the growing season I continue to add mulch, so that it remains 8 to 12 inches thick around the plants. The tubers develop in this thick mulch.

Pruning Recommended

Before mulching, prune each plant back to one stem if you want large baking potatoes. Two stems will give you a mixture of bakers and medium-size potatoes. With three or more stems the plants will tend to produce only small to medium tubers.

It helps if seed potatoes are "greened" before planting. Spread the seed potato sections in a bright, but not sunny, area—such as an enclosed porch—for 2 to 3 weeks. Through exposure to the light the potatoes will green up a little. At the same time the cut sections will dry off, making them less susceptible to rotting in the ground. Should they begin to sprout in this period, so much the better.

When planting sprouted potatoes, see that all but the tips of the sprouts are covered with compost or soil.

How to Add Water

Water once a week during hot, dry weather. After removing the nozzle, I push the end of the hose into the mulch next to each plant and hold it there for about 10 seconds. This way I can be sure that the water gets where it's needed—to the roots. A wet mulch on a dry soil is the last thing you want. When checking to see if the potatoes need water, look at the soil under the mulch, not at the mulch.

Harvest early potatoes by feeling in the mulch and removing a few for a special taste treat. Dig up the rest after the blossoms have gone by, or leave the plants in the ground until the tops begin to die off. After lifting the potatoes, leave them exposed to the sun for 2 days to allow the skins to harden off. Don't leave them longer, or they may begin to turn green.

Plant early varieties (80 days) for a summer harvest; late varieties (120 days) for a fall crop. Check with your extension agent or local seed merchants for the varieties that do best in your area.

Conventional Planting

The more conventional way to grow potatoes is to plant them 3 inches deep in a furrow 6 inches deep. When the young plants have grown up above the level of the furrow, fill it in with soil; continue to draw soil up around the stems for the next few weeks. Finally, cover the soil mounds with an organic mulch to keep the soil cool and moist.

Compost and leaves provide all the nutrients in my potato patch. Some gardeners lightly sprinkle a general-purpose fertilizer in the furrows where the potatoes are planted; others add it in narrow bands on each side of the rows. Avoid fresh manure as this tends to give potatoes rough skins.

What if you haven't enough garden space for potatoes? Getting around this problem might require a little ingenuity. Bushel baskets filled with compost or soil and placed in a reasonably sunny corner of a patio, porch, or roof can yield a meal or two of fresh potatoes for your family.

Auto tires can be put to use, as mentioned earlier. I've read of one gardener who converted a rocky area into a potato patch by placing used auto tires in twos, one on top of the other, and filling them with compost. For potatoes "it's the only way to grow," he insists.

If you use containers, watch that they do not get too hot during the height of summer. A piece of cloth draped loosely around the container is usually enough to take care of the problem.

By the way, tests in Britain have shown that potatoes respond very well to fertilization with liquid seaweed. Yields have increased quite remarkably in many instances.

Volunteer Vine Inspires Sugar Pumpkin Crop

Last year a volunteer pumpkin sprang up right where it shouldn't, in a bed given over to summer carrots.

It should have been whipped out just as soon as it appeared. As gardeners more disciplined than I are wont to put it, "a plant out of place is a weed." But I let it stay, anyway, and in the end it rewarded us with two of the sweetest pumpkins ever.

I let it grow in the only space available—right up the center of an adjoining path—and vigorously pruned away all side shoots. Because it was a late starter, the vine had produced only two fruits by the time the cooler weather of September made it advisable to trim the end off the vine and curtail its ramblings altogether.

In the past I have tended to avoid pumpkins, despite what they did for Cinderella and still do for Halloween. Instead, I've concentrated on winter squash because of their finer-textured flesh and better taste, or so I thought before those sugar pumpkins turned up on the dinner plate.

I'd been given a few seeds of the smallest member of the pumpkin clan, and when I felt I wouldn't use them, I consigned them to the shredder. One seed, it seems, must have escaped intact and sprouted after some compost was tilled into the soil.

As a result of that experience, I plan on a pumpkin patch this year. It will contain the sugar pumpkins that grow to between 6 and 7 inches across. They make delicious pies, breads, soups, muffins, and just about every other dish pumpkins or winter squash are used in. We baked one of ours last year and boiled the other—and to our surprise found them as tasty as squash.

Pumpkins, like squash, produce moderately on moderate soil but in great abundance in rich, fertile soil. One of the easiest methods of enriching the soil is to dig a hole, fill it with a shovelful or two of compost and/or manure, and top with about 2 inches of soil. Plant about five seeds in each of these hills. Thin to two plants per hill, and space each hill 8 feet apart.

In gardening terms a hill means a place where several seeds are planted in a clump rather than singly or in rows. It doesn't mean a raised mound of soil. Indeed, in my garden most hills are valleys.

I make them in depressions, so that water flows toward the roots and not away from them every time it rains. This is important because my garden soil drains easily, and summers here in the Boston area tend to be on the dry side. In wet areas, where soil drainage may be slow, stay on the level and avoid depression planting.

Once the cooler weather moves in, remove the fuzzy tip of each vine to end further plant growth and steer all plant nutrients into maturing the more recently formed fruits.

When frost threatens in the fall, cover the pumpkins with a blanket or something similar. You've brought them this far, and you don't want them damaged by the cold. James Whitcomb Riley wrote the well-known, "When the frost is on the punkin," but good gardeners try never to let that happen.

Year-Round Garden Supplies Yule Rutabaga

When we journeyed to Florida to celebrate Christmas with friends not long ago, we included a rutabaga among the presents we packed in the trunk.

We dug it from under the mulch the day before we left, and when it was trimmed top and bottom, it weighed more than 5 pounds. My wife had suggested substituting two of more modest proportions, but I wanted to show it off.

We enjoyed it for Christmas dinner, and it was as sweet and mild-tasting on the plate as it had been good-looking in the garden—

as were all the dozens or so rutabagas, or Swede turnips, we have grown.

I had sown the seed in richly manured soil around the middle of July and had found they continue to grow well after the first light frosts of the season came along. What I particularly liked about them was that they can be stored out in the garden, along with carrots, parsnips, and sometimes beets, under a heavy mulch all winter long.

In July there are several vegetables that can be planted for a fall and winter harvest. Besides rutabagas, these include beets, carrots, Chinese cabbage, kale, radishes, and spinach. Among frost-tender crops, bush beans can be sown up to the middle of August for a pre-frost crop in most areas. Even early sweet corn, sown then, has a better than even chance of producing mature cobs.

In preparing the soil dig liberal quantities of manure and/or compost into the top 3 or 4 inches of soil. I aim for the equivalent of a 1-inch thick covering. Be less generous with extrarich manures, such as chicken or rabbit.

If you use commercial fertilizer, sprinkle 4 pounds of 5-10-10 over 100 square feed of garden. Add some compost too, as experience suggests that the fertilizer is partly absorbed by the organic matter and released more steadily to the plants. Water well and often during the hot weeks of summer until the seedlings are well established.

I have used shredded leaves about 2 feet deep, sometimes combined with bags of leaves, as a mulch in order to store hardy root crops in the ground all winter long. This practice, which I first read about in *Organic Gardening* magazine almost ten years ago, has been gaining converts steadily. Recently, I have heard of northern gardeners who mulched heavily with leaves topped by a plastic sheet. This makes considerable sense to me because not only does the plastic offer additional insulation but it also opens up the possibility of using newspaper as a mulch.

Newspaper is one of the most effective insulators you can find anywhere—until it gets wet. So let the newspaper provide the insulation while the plastic keeps it dry. You might even try filling plastic trash bags with newspapers to form small blankets 1 to 2 inches thick. These can be thrown on top of other mulches, both to keep them in place and to add extra insulation.

Be assured there are few more rewarding gardening experiences than to go outdoors in the middle of January and dig up the bulk of the evening's dinner.

How Kitchen Waste Boosts Squash Harvest

To my wife's delight—and my younger daughter's disgust—our small garden has given us 170 pounds of winter squash this season.

That's roughly double last year's production, enough for a whole season of hearty dinners and who knows how many squash pies (which my daughter loves only because she doesn't know squash is the major ingredient).

To get this increased production we extended our garden a little. But a happy accident helped, too.

This year we grew tomatoes by a method attributed to the Japanese—by filling wire-enclosed circles with garden refuse and then planting the tomatoes around these minicompost heaps. The effect of this method on tomato production was very satisfying indeed. On the other hand, its contribution to squash production was nothing short of exciting to me.

Among the refuse we piled into these tomato circles were the peelings, and some seeds apparently, of butternut squash. These promptly grew with such vigor that they soon threatened the tomatoes. I had no choice but to pull up most of them. Two of them, though, were allowed to stay after I had trained them through the tomatoes and left them to trail down a path—the only open space left in the garden.

Now elsewhere in the garden the butternuts grew to an average and satisfying size for the breed—around 2 to 3 pounds apiece. But those two vines, with their roots in pure compost, produced six squash weighing between 4½ to almost 6 pounds each.

So already I am preparing for next year's squash garden. In the middle of it is a circle of wire, some 4 feet across, into which will go garden waste and shredded leaves to a height of maybe 4 feet. Next season, I will plant the squash seeds directly in this pile and let the vines trail out from there. The beauty of squash vines is that they thrive even in only partly decomposed compost.

I plant bush squash—both summer and winter varieties—in hills roughly 3 feet apart each way. I dig out a shovelful of earth, replace it with compost, and top this with an inch of soil in which I sow six seeds 1 inch deep. When the seeds are up and growing, I thin them to three plants to a hill. Later I add more compost as mulch, 1 inch or more thick and perhaps 18 inches in diameter. Substitute old manure for compost, if you wish.

Sometimes I grow vining types the same way, though I dig much deeper holes, which are half filled with raw garbage before being topped with mature compost and soil.

If space is a problem you might try growing these squash up a fence. The resulting squash will not be quite as large because the fence approach does not allow the vine to send down auxiliary roots as it does when it crawls on the ground. Compensate for this by additional compost or manure (or both) in the hills, and feed it regularly with liquid manure.

I've also grown Hubbard squash up a fence, but these much-larger fruit must be cradled in a sling or their weight will damage the vine.

Harvest zucchini and summer squash when they are no more than 2 inches in diameter, and the patty-pan types when 3 to 4 inches across. In contrast, winter squash must be allowed to mature on the vine. When harvesting, always leave an inch or more of the stalk attached to winter squash. This is important if the squash is to store well.

If the weather is warm, leave them out in the sun to further harden the skin. Finally, give them the fingernail test. If you press down on the skin with your nail and it does not break, the squash is mature enough to store. If it does give way under the pressure of your nail, then make sure you eat that particular squash early on. It will still taste good.

Try Sweet Potatoes—in the Garden and on the Menu

A letter arrived from a friend in Alaska the other day. After telling us about Kodiak bears, king crabs, and the like, she suddenly announced that she had "discovered the delights of baked sweet potatoes."

We rejoiced with her because we made the same discovery many years ago. The fact is sweet potatoes can be baked, boiled, fried, steamed, you name it, and they always taste great. They are one of only a few vegetables that can fill every slot on the menu from soup through dessert. One recipe pamphlet lists eleven different sweet potato puddings and, would you believe, sweet potato custard!

American Indians were cultivating this vegetable along with corn centuries before the arrival of Columbus. The seafaring Spaniards took it to the Philippines, from which it quickly spread through the South Seas to New Zealand, Australia, and on to Africa.

In the United States it got its big push when George Washington discovered its delightful flavor and instructed that it be planted in his Mount Vernon garden every year. It still is. Noting this, enterprising nurserymen suggested growing "sweets" in the backyard (or even on the windowsill, since it makes an attractive houseplant) to celebrate the bicentennial.

I first grew sweet potatoes in the subtropics, an ideal climate for this heat-loving plant, but I was wary of trying them in New England until a few years ago. The growing season was too short, I felt.

But by growing a few in warm, protected areas of the garden I was able to raise enough for two or three family meals. Now, however, I have hopes of a much better crop. The answer lies in a short-seasoned variety called Centennial.

I learned about it when I got to talking with Dudley Sanders the other day. He is a schoolteacher and long-time sweet potato grower from Gleason, Tennessee. The Centennial, he tells me, was developed by Dr. Julian Miller at Louisiana State University about a decade ago. It is a dark orange, very sweet "tater" that develops to a marketable (baby baker, says Mr. Sanders) size in just 90 days. Given a longer season it will grow as large as any other variety.

It used to be said that it was not worth growing sweets farther north than the southern part of New Jersey. But in recent years Centennial has helped change all that. Just as new breeds over the years have pushed corn ever northward into Canada, so the Centennial has made reasonable sweet-potato harvests possible in the north nowadays.

In the colder states Mr. Sanders suggests planting the sweets the first week in June.

"Let a little heat get into the soil," he says, "so the plants can start taking off right away." That should give them three hot months to grow before troublesome frosts come along.

Sweets grow best in light, well-drained soil. It helps to plant them in ridges, raised 6 or more inches above the surrounding beds. This benefits the sweets in several ways. The soil warms up more quickly, drains better, and tends to stay loose enough for the tubers to develop well.

Mix some well-rotted compost or leaf mold into the soil. Otherwise, use a light application of general fertilizer. Avoid a fertilizer with a high nitrogen content as this will result in large tops and spindly tubers.

Set the young plants 1 foot apart in rows 3½ feet apart. This allows the trailing vines some room to spread. On the other hand, you can save space, as you might with cucumbers and other trailing vines, by growing them on a fence or trellis.

Once the plants are growing well, water applied at the base of the ridge will be quite satisfactory. Until then, sprinkle the ridges gently, making sure the soil is dampened right through.

Caged Tomato Plants Produce Bountiful Crop

I've come to the conclusion that the best and most convenient way to grow tomatoes is to cage them—to fence them in and leave them to do their thing.

Simply plant your tomato the usual way; then surround it with a tube or cage made of reinforced concrete wire, pig netting, or other wire fencing with holes wide enough for you to put your arm through. Step back and watch the plant take off, filling the cage with luxuriant, fruit-producing growth.

Last season I caged part of my tomato crop for the first time, and the results were good enough for me to extend the practice this year to all, including the shorter determinate varieties.

Less Pruning, Tying

One obvious advantage to the cage method is that it cuts down on time-consuming pruning, staking, and tying throughout the growing season. It also increases the per-plant yield—and that's not just my one-season observation but that of gardeners who have been raising tomatoes this way for several years.

Central Ohio gardener Bob Saunders is one of these. He's had yields of up to 200 tomatoes from one plant. Compare that with the 30-tomato average for most staked plants. Last year he harvested 1,400 tomatoes—"many over one pound each," he says—from just eight plants.

Naturally, there is much more to getting bushels of tomatoes than a simple wire cage. So let's start from the beginning.

About eight weeks before I plan to set out my tomatoes I sow seeds indoors in flats or starter blocks and leave them to grow under fluorescent lights (a sunny window would be just as good).

At 4 to 6 inches tall, I transplant them into containers, such as Styrofoam cups; and finally, when 8 to 10 inches tall, they go into half-gallon milk cartons or similar tall containers.

Deep-Planting Benefits

Now the tomato is the one plant that not only tolerates deep planting but benefits from it. So with each transplanting I drop the root ball to the bottom of the larger container and fill it with potting soil up to the plant's neck, so to speak—within two or three sets of leaves from the top. In a matter of days the now-buried stem will have sent out new roots, thus strengthening the root system immensely.

In late April, here in Massachusetts, I begin digging the holes (19 inches separating each hole) where the tomatoes will be set out. They are roughly 18 inches in diameter and 18 inches deep. At this stage I frequently throw hot dishwater in each hole to help warm up the still-cold soil. I also cover each hole with a sheet of clear plastic or an old glass window pane to create a greenhouse effect in the hole and further warm up the soil.

Enriching the Soil

Next, I half fill each hole with compost or a manure-soil mixture (be sure the manure is old), to which may be added a handful of bone meal and rock phosphate. Then, 2 or 3 weeks before it is considered safe to set out frost-tender tomatoes, mine are planted in the holes so that the tops are a good 6 inches from the plastic or glass covering. In these miniature "sun pits," the plants, protected from cold spring winds, enjoy a warm summerlike environment.

A word of caution here: On bright, sunny days move the plastic back a small fraction (as you would raise the lid of a cold frame) to let the excess heat escape. Cover the hole again at night.

As the plants grow, fill in around the stem with soil. If the weather is still too cold when the plants grow up out of the hole, replace the plastic with a gallon plastic milk jug with the bottom cut out and the cap removed. This will continue the greenhouse effect for a week or so longer.

Another option, mentioned earlier, is to place an old tire on the ground, fill it with the compost mixture, and plant the tomato in that. Now place a second tire on top of the first, and cover with plastic or glass. In effect you now have an aboveground sun pit. It works just as well.

Making the Cages

Finally, give the tomatoes their cages. Mr. Saunders makes his out of reinforced concrete wire (look up in the yellow pages under concrete supplies). He counts off ten squares (5 feet) of the reinforcing wire and cuts down through the center of the next square. Then he bends and crimps these 3-inch extensions to hold the 18-inch-diameter ring in place.

Hold the cage in place by tying it to a stake driven into the ground or by cutting out the bottom horizontal ring and pushing the resulting vertical spikes into the ground for anchorage.

Once the soil has thoroughly warmed up, I mulch heavily to conserve moisture and prevent the surface roots from being damaged by the overheated soil. In the cooler days of late summer, the mulch keeps the soil heat locked in to extend the plants' growth. Water heavily once a week in dry weather.

Now you can sit back and wait for what should be an abundant harvest.

How to Double Your Tomato Yield—the Japanese Way

A friend whose expertise with a camera has taken him to more than eighty countries around the world returned one year with an interesting idea on tomato culture.

He got it from the Japanese, and after he'd tried it out here in New England, he knew the Land of the Rising Sun had scored again. "They claimed it boosted tomato production tremendously from each bush," he said. "It doubled my garden's production," he added.

The method is a simple one: Take standard fencing wire 3 to 4 feet high, and make a circle 3 to 5 feet in diameter. Fill this wire enclosure with any compost material—grass, leaves, weeds, food waste, a little manure (if you have it), and every so often a sprinkling of soil. Plant your tomatoes around this circle, as many as you have room for. I keep mine about 2 feet apart.

Fill the bottom of the wire circle with well-rotted compost and manure, and perhaps a little bone meal, to a depth of about 6 inches. After that it doesn't much matter how fresh the material is. It will decompose pretty readily during the season.

The tomatoes will quickly send their roots under and even into this circle of compost in the making. Here the soil will stay relatively cool during the hot months of summer, moist and constantly enriched by a steady flow of nutrients from above.

Finally, when the season is over, when you've eaten your fill of the red, vine-ripened fruit and preserved as juice or paste a whole lot more, those wire circles will present a gold mine of black, crumbly, compost all ready to spread over and enrich another vegetable bed. Then re-erect those circles and start all over again.

Don't Turn Up Your Nose at Rhubarb

It was a moment of sweet triumph for my wife.

"John," she exulted to a friend of mine, "you have just eaten rhubarb!" And indeed he had. Moreover, he had confessed to liking it.

But let me explain. Several years at a Dickensian boarding school for boys in his youth had eradicated any like he ever had for *Rheum rhaponticum*, to give its botanical name. Both plentiful and cheap, he claims it appeared on the school menu without fail almost every day. "Stewed rhubarb, ugh," he recalled with a shudder.

Yet here he was confessing to liking a baked confection whose principal ingredient was rhubarb. A type of sweet bread, it has become a favorite of mine ever since my wife discovered the recipe in a Maine cookbook.

That's the beauty of rhubarb. Besides serving it as a sauce (so cool and refreshing on a hot summer day), it can be combined with so many other fruits in a variety of cakes, pies, breads, and jams. (Would you believe rhubarb, crushed pineapple, and a packet of strawberry gelatin makes great "strawberry" jam!)

In other words, any gardener who grows it can get a great deal of mileage out of rhubarb. In fact my wife considers the ten crowns I bought in the spring of 1973 to be "one of our best gardening investments."

We took only a very few stalks from the newly planted crowns the first year while they established themselves, but after that we harvested a veritable forest of thick, red, juicy stalks. They have grown more productive every year.

We pick rhubarb through the first or second week of July. After that, tempting though the stalks may appear, we leave them alone. The food the leaves produce through the balance of the growing season will be stored in the crowns to produce the flush of tender stalks we will relish next spring.

Rhubarb is a heavy feeder. The more fertilizer and compost you give it, the more vigorous and plentiful the supply of stalks. It will grow in most types of soil, too, provided it is well drained.

Dig a hole about the size of bushel basket where each crown will be planted. Then throw in a shovelful each of well-rotted manure and compost, if you have it. After that return the top soil to the hole, and mix in more compost, if available.

When I planted my rhubarb I was somewhat short of both manure and compost. I managed less than a trowelful of each per plant. But I did have shredded leaves, and after planting I spread a 2-inch layer over the entire bed. The results proved most satisfactory. The leaves disintegrated, slowly feeding the plants while keeping the bed cool and moist.

Spring or fall planting is generally recommended, though I know of one gardener who got his rhubarb patch started with a mid-summer planting. After preparing the holes, plant the crowns about 2 inches deep. Then see they don't go thirsty.

Each July I feed my rhubarb with a bucketful per plant of compost. Then in the fall, when the plants have died back, I put them to bed for the winter by covering them with a blanket of shredded leaves 2 to 3 inches thick.

Established rhubarb can be harvested for 4 to 6 years before they need digging up and dividing. I plan on dividing a couple of plants each year. No sense in waiting until they all have to be done en masse.

Meanwhile, if you are planning to introduce rhubarb into your garden, start collecting recipes, too.

Raspberries, Red and Black, and How to Grow Them

Nearly every morning my wife spreads raspberry jam on her slice of breakfast toast. Sometimes she makes raspberry jam tarts, and occasionally turnovers, so hot that the jam is still boiling when it comes to the table.

The jam is homemade. And the raspberries are homegrown. I always marvel at how productive a small raspberry patch can be.

In his *Fruits and Berries for the Home Garden,* Lewis Hill has this to say: "Raspberries are one of the easiest crops to grow. Usually you can get a big crop the third year after planting and after that be certain of continuous crops year after year—sometimes for nearly a lifetime. They produce abundantly; we figure a foot of row produces a pint of berries during the season."

But even though raspberries—and that other popular bramble, the blackberry—grow so easily, there are a few basic needs that must be met to ensure good harvests.

These are a weed-free soil that is also free of tree roots, good drainage, and vigorous pruning to keep the plants from smothering themselves.

By far the most popular bramble is the red raspberry. One-crop and two-crop varieties are available. The first bears in midsummer on canes grown the previous year; the latter also bears in summer and again in the fall on the tips of canes grown that same year.

Plant raspberries 2 feet apart in rows 4 to 5 feet apart. Set them out as deep as they grew in the nursery. If you buy potted plants, these will need no pruning at planting time. On the other hand, barerooted mail order stock should be pruned back to about 3 inches after being set out. This will encourage the development of a sturdy new root system.

Water every few days for the first two weeks, by which time new growth should have begun. Mulch to discourage weeds and to maintain moisture and even soil temperatures.

Some growers string a wire between two poles about 3½ feet above the ground and fasten the canes to this. Others string two wires 30 inches apart and let the canes grow up between them. A third method is to stake each individual bush, loosely tying the canes to the stake.

Brambles readily sucker and will quickly spread into the paths if unchecked. Pull up all these unwanted suckers, or else remove them by running a rotary lawnmower between the rows.

While pruning is highly important, it is straightforward. In the spring remove all weak or damaged canes at ground level. Also remove any dead two-year-old canes that you may have missed the previous fall. Finally, thin out the remaining canes to about 6 inches apart.

In the fall cut out all two-year-old canes that fruited in the summer, and trim back the remaining canes to about 4½ feet.

Black raspberries grow differently from the red, as they send out side shoots from the upright canes. When the tips of black raspberry canes touch the ground they will root. In pruning, top all main canes at about 2½ feet in height, and trim back the side shoots to 6 inches from the main cane. Because of this different growth habit, black raspberry canes should be thinned each spring to about 12 inches apart.

Blackberries grow similarly to black raspberries (though the flavor is quite distinct) and require similar treatment. Trailing blackberries, sometimes called dewberries, on the other hand, grow as long, slender canes that trail over the ground. Cut these back to about 4½ feet in height, and attach them to a wire strand.

Be careful to remove all prunings from the area, as pests can winter over in the dead stalks. Most authorities recommend burning these prunings as a sanitary measure. I shred mine and incorporate them in a compost pile that I know will get good and hot.

Bramble fruits can be damaged by too much fertilizer. But an early spring feeding will help. Just before growth begins, lightly sprinkle a balanced fertilizer (between 5 and 10 pounds per 100 feet of row) over the canes and on the mulched paths between the rows. Do this only when the canes are dry.

It is important to keep the paths as well as the immediate row area mulched, for the roots of brambles spread out 2 feet and more each way. The organic mulch will feed the brambles as it slowly breaks down. So if a mulch is added each year, spring fertilizing can slowly be reduced and ultimately discontinued altogether.

Backyard Strawberry Patch Needs Water, Sun, and Care

The botanists call it *Fragaria*. But long ago those who cultivated it extensively found that straw mulches so improved the harvest that they gave it the common name of strawberry.

It is native to the United States, but long before the colonists and George III stopped speaking to each other the strawberry had found its way to Europe—and from there to much of the world.

In the process it has become a thoroughly international little berry, fruiting as generously in Australia and Africa as it does in America. The English, who are rightfully proud of the specimens they produce, are particularly fond of the off-season berries they get from Kenya.

Over the years skillful breeders have developed varieties that thrive in Alaska and others that revel in the humid heat of Florida. In other words, no matter where you live there are probably varieties that will suit your region.

Little wonder, then, that the strawberry has become the most widely grown of all berry fruits and, given the right conditions, is probably the most productive per square foot of growing space.

Strawberries need a sunny location and a rich humus-filled soil. So dig or till generous quantities of manure and/or compost into the top 12 inches of the bed. Remember, the strawberry is shallow-rooted, and while it can survive dry periods, it cannot do so and still produce fruit. The organic material you add to your soil is, therefore, as important for its moisture-holding qualities as for the plant nutrients it supplies.

Figuring How Many

Reckon on twenty-five plants per person if you want a goodly supply of fresh berries, plus some left over for freezing and preserves.

Given a spacious garden it is still best to go with conventional flat-bed planting. But in cramped yards, vertical plantings, such as strawberry barrels and hanging baskets, may be the answer to your strawberry-filled future. Another approach is to mix strawberries in with flowers in the garden. Or you might plant them as an edging along a path.

Whatever the method, it is most important to set out strawberries at the correct depth; the crown, or thick portion of the plant, should be level with the soil. The crown may rot if covered with soil, while too shallow a planting can dry out the roots.

There are two commonly accepted approaches to planting strawberries—the matted row and hill methods.

In the former, strawberries are set out in the spring, 18 to 24 inches apart in rows 2½ to 3 feet apart. These are then allowed to multiply freely by means of runners so that soon the whole bed is a matted mass of plants. It is best to limit the number of runners to six per plant.

Commercial growers generally set out new plants in the spring, harvest a heavy crop of berries the following spring, and then plow in the plants and begin all over again. In my own experience the home gardener can take at least two or three annual harvests before replanting.

Some gardeners plant one bed of strawberries one year and harvest it the next. Then they set out new plants in a second bed. After harvesting the first bed they till in the old plants and plant nitrogen-fixing green beans. In the fall they plow in the beans, and the bed is ready for another planting of strawberries the following spring. This way they both harvest and plant strawberries every year.

In the hill method, strawberries are set out 9 to 12 inches apart, and all runners are cut off immediately after they begin to form. The pruning process is constant, and because the plants use up no energy producing new ones, they remain vigorously productive for up to 6 years.

Of all strawberries, those that bear just once a year are the most productive. These are known as spring or June bearers and are the only ones grown by commercial producers.

With these it is important to remove all flowers that form during the year they were planted so that all energy goes into plant growth for a big crop the following June.

The everbearing varieties yield fruit in the spring and again in the fall with an occasional berry in between. However, the season-long production of the everbearer seldom matches the spring crop of the June bearer. A fall crop can be taken from the everbearers during the same year of planting.

Weeding a Must

Weeds are one of the strawberry's worst foes. So weed assiduously, or else use a mulch. I mulch with shredded leaves, tucking them under the strawberry leaves to keep down the weeds and also to maintain even soil temperature and moisture. You can use straw, fibrous compost, composted horse manure, or even wood chips if you wish.

In the fall, when temperatures begin to drop consistently below 25°F at night, add an additional mulch of straw over the top of the plants. This prevents possible winter damage. In the spring, carefully remove the straw mulch when new growth begins. Do this on an overcast day so that the tender shoots are not suddenly exposed to the heat of the sun.

During the growing season give strawberries the equivalent of 1 inch of rain each week. From the time flowers begin to form until shortly before harvest, once-a-week applications of half-strength liquid fertilizer or manure or compost "tea" are most beneficial.

Late-spring frosts are dangerous. While the plant is frost-resistant, its flowers are not. So when frost threatens and your strawberry beds are a mass of white flowers, cover them with burlap, old sheets, newspaper, or plastic. A light spray of water running all night will also do the trick.

Alpine Strawberries—a Great Border Plant

A friend of mine, perhaps because his background is Austrian or possibly because his Yankee wife thought it a good idea, raised some Alpine strawberries from seed several years back.

It was an eminently successful venture, providing him with an annual taste treat that isn't available in stores or restaurants this side of Paris, where the French call them *fraises des bois* (fraze-day-bwah). Fortunately, both seeds and plants are available in the United States, which should make a lot of discriminating gardeners happy.

Not everyone takes immediately to the wild strawberry flavor, but as Amos Pettingill puts it in his 1981 *Garden Book,* the high-quality catalog of White Flower Farm, Litchfield, Connecticut: "The first spoonful might even be a disappointment, but not the third. That addicts."

My friend, who since leaving Massachusetts a few years ago has taken to raising Alpine strawberries on Florida's west coast, contends he didn't need that many spoonfuls. One was enough. The flavor does differ from the commercial berries we buy in the stores here. But it is delectable while still being distinctly strawberry.

Unlike the conventional strawberry, Alpines do not creep. In other words, they do not send out runners, but should be divided every third year. Two to five new plants come from every division, which means that a few can readily develop into a large berry patch. Because of this growth habit, the berries make a great edging plant around walks or around larger flower beds.

Put another way, Alpines aren't just for the backyard garden anymore. They can be used wherever the ornamental effect is needed. Along with the beauty there will always be the berries.

Alpine berries are pointed in shape and smaller than conventional strawberries. Established plants begin bearing around the end of June and continue until frost. This means a summer-long supply of the fruit for every household that has them.

Flowers are borne on moderately long stems, but the berries that follow have a way of hiding beneath the leaves. You may have to hunt for ripe berries, but the harvest is worth the search. This growth habit also means that there are often more ripe berries to be had than you think.

The plants are fairly prolific, too. My friend and neighbor would often pick a bowlful of the berries one day, and three days later he'd need to pick again. As with many everbearing plants, keeping the berries picked encourages the plants to produce more.

Plant the Alpine strawberries in fertile, well-prepared soil that does not hold puddles of water after a heavy rain. Set out the young plants on 12-inch centers. In the colder regions of the country set out plants in the spring; in warmer regions both fall as well as spring planting is feasible. As they are vulnerable to frost heaving, see that the plants are protected by a mulch wherever ground freezing occurs.

Sow seeds indoors about 6 weeks before the last heavy frost in your region, barely covering them with moist potting soil. A clear plastic bag placed around the seed tray helps maintain the right germinating conditions. Be sure to use only transparent plastic, as strawberry seeds are light-responsive, meaning that germination is triggered by light as well as moisture and warm temperatures. Seedlings should sprout within 14 to 21 days. If possible, grow them in a slightly cooler situation (60 to 65°F), but this is not vital.

When the seedlings have two pairs of leaves or more, transplant them into individual containers ready for setting out in the garden after all frost danger is past. Meanwhile, be sure to condition them gently to the outdoors by placing them in a cold frame or by placing them outdoors for short periods before bringing them back indoors.

Afterword

From the time when I began to garden more or less seriously, I was always eager to try my hand at something new. It might be an innovative technique picked up from a fellow gardener, or one that suggested itself from my own experience. If the new technique worked, I'd stick with it, otherwise I'd drop it and try another approach.

My years as a roving reporter for *The Christian Science Monitor* brought me into contact with many useful ideas for gardening. This book contains all those that worked well for me. May they now inspire you to develop your own unique approach to working with the soil.

P. T.

Notes